Redeemed

Joselyn Joaquín de Jenkins

Published by Hemingway Publishers

Cover design by Hemingway Publishers

ISBN: Printed in the United States

HEMINGWAY
PUBLISHERS

Table of Content

FORWARD

When I started reading Sister Joselyn Joaquín's book, I was impressed. Her story reflects the reality that many families live.

There are situations of dysfunctional homes full of abuse, and so many challenges that mark the lives of kids, young people and entire families. Still, it is evident in her history how God heals, frees and marks us for life and can change our entire history as the Word says. This book must reach every life that has gone through these situations or is going through them because it is full of hope for those who feel immersed in traumas and damages created in the heart of the family and find a way out that is in Christ Jesus.

Pastor Jorge Alejandro Vásquez Javier

Professional broadcaster, law graduate, family therapy technician, and pastor for more than 14 years at the Christian Church of Grace, Santo Domingo, DR.

This book is a powerful testimony of God's grace amidst pain. I don't think I have read someone who, with as much honesty and courage as Joselyn, shares her story not only as a reminder of the struggles she has overcome, but as a beacon of hope for those still seeking healing and purpose. From the first page, she invites us to remember that God's love transforms and renews, bringing strength to those who have faced suffering. This book is more than a personal story; it is a guide of hope for any wounded heart. Step in and receive healing.

Dr. Jonatan S. Gómez A.

Apostle of the Church House of King Jesus and the Gosen Apostolic Network. Santo Domingo, Dominican Republic.

The story you have in your hands is a story of a brave and hardworking woman who has lived through many processes, struggles, and challenges, reflecting the impact that childhood wounds do in our decisions and in the way we interact with others, which, if we are not aware and do not heal, can affect our lives in ways we never imagined. This book not only tells the story of a woman who lived through difficult experiences, but also how God heals and transforms her wounds. The Word of God says that: *He heals the broken-hearted, sets the captive free, and delivers the prisoners from captivity,*

Isaiah 61:1.

Every one of you will find in these pages something meaningful, something that can change your life.

I have known Joselyn since 2004. I can say that her life has been a process of transformation and constant learning, and growing. Despite the different and hard circumstances she has gone through, her faith and love for God have remained.

I invite you to read with your heart, to let yourself be carried away by the words and to discover how God's immense love transforms our lives.

Even if your sins are like red on fire, you will be as white as snow. Isaiah 1:18

Susana Tamarez

Family Therapist Santo Domingo, RD

Dedication

I dedicate this book to Him who inspired me to write it—He who is my Rock, my Strength, and my Peace—my Lord and Saviour, Jesus Christ. His grace has been enough for me, and today I write and testify of His love, mercy, grace, and power. Thank You, my Father, for Your eternal love and compassion toward us. Thanks be to the Holy Spirit, who guides us to the Truth. He supports us in times of need and continues to encourage us until we see Jesus face-to-face.

I dedicate this book also to my children, their descendants, and future generations, so that they may carry a legacy of knowing who the Lord Jesus Christ is, what He can do in our lives, and of His great love for each of us. I pray they will have the courage to believe and accept His love, confident that He loves them and has a good plan for them, not an evil one. I love you, my children. You are valuable, loved, and precious in God's and my eyes, I bless you.

I dedicate this book to my husband, Donald, who is a blessing to me and all of our families on both sides.

I also dedicate this book to everyone who has been hurt, abused, used, and rejected, so they can remember that their lives can be transformed, and a better tomorrow is possible. I dedicate this book to those who struggle to find healing and deliverance but feel far from God. I also dedicate it to all those who are in the faith but face great struggles in their flesh and minds, who may sometimes have thoughts of giving up. No matter how far you've gone wrong or how much you've fallen, there is always a chance to shake yourself off, get up, turn around, and start anew.

I dedicate this book to you, my dear reader, with love.

INTRODUCTIONS

Thank you for choosing to read my book. This has been God's project for me for many years, but now is the time to share it. I can write about many topics, but this is what God first placed on my heart, and I have responded in obedience. I've heard many say, "Let's not talk about the past anymore. The past is over." Indeed, it has already happened, and the past does not determine our future. If I am willing to leave it behind, I become a witness to new beginnings. I have been regenerated and transformed. Yet, I understand that we overcome by sharing our stories; in doing so, we also find greater healing and freedom, and others can discover comfort and hope when we are genuine and vulnerable.

My greatest desire in writing this is to give glory to my Heavenly Father and to encourage the one who reads it to have faith, hope, and strength.

Writing this book has brought me healing and an even deeper deliverance from a traumatic and painful past that shaped my life. The past no longer defines me, but many need a living example of firsthand experience to encourage and strengthen them. In this book, I mention my natural father, whom I loved. I mention him not to highlight his mistakes or weaknesses, but because he is part of my history, my life, and my reality. To share my life story, it is necessary to acknowledge his role in it. I have learned that we are to honour our father and mother, and I do not intend to demean his life or his memory in the hearts of those who esteemed him.

I mention other people as well because they have been a genuine part of my story, not to highlight their mistakes or to belittle them either. We have all failed. I put myself first, and we all need God's forgiveness and mercy every single day. God only knows how difficult it has been for me to write this book, and how many tears I have shed that caused me to stop writing, only to pick it up again later. I have cried, prayed, laughed, and experienced even deeper healing and deliverance as I wrote it. Being vulnerable brings us healing and freedom.

"In Your Hands" is a true story that moves from a very traumatic childhood filled with violence, fears, insecurities, uncertainties, rejections, traumas, and toxic conflicts, to a life not defined by the natural but by the supernatural, where I am no longer a victim but more than a victor.

You, too, are called to win and have victory in life, regardless of everything and in whatever season of life you are in. I pray that my story will help you gain new strength and courage if you need it, and that you can move forward.

Chapter 1
A Very Difficult Childhood

I was the first of eleven children, born to my father and mother. My father had more than twenty children altogether with different women.

I have some very hard memories of my childhood. One of them I remember is from when I was about four or five years old. I ran to my neighbours, who lived across the alley from our house in Rio Verde (a section of a province in the DR). My father came to look for me with a belt in his hands. When I saw him coming, I hid under a table. He grabbed me very furiously, pulled me out, slapped me, hit me with a belt, and then took me back home by the arm. I cried and trembled with fear; I was very small.

I remember seeing my father approaching my mother many times with the slightest excuse, usually out of jealousy. He used to see shadows of what he imagined my mother was doing wrong, and out of nowhere, he began to beat her—with his fists, sometimes with whatever he could grab: a belt, a piece of wood, or anything within reach—leaving her bruised, her face full of sobs, tears, and marks.

When we moved to another house in El Mirador, Moca, I usually played with the neighbours in front of our home, always aware and afraid that my dad might come or pass by and find out that I was playing or visiting our neighbours, and that would start a war.

There was no television in our house, and my siblings and I would go to watch cartoons at our neighbours' house after school, but we were afraid that my father would find out, scold us, and beat us. We were also afraid to ask him for permission to go, because we knew—at least in our minds—

that he would say no or get upset about it.

My father was a good friend to his friends and a hardworking man. He liked to drink and was very womanizing, jealous, suspicious, irascible, violent, and aggressive. He was very nice and friendly on the streets, but at home with us, he was different—at least in my house.

He drank heavily, sometimes for days. When he got drunk, his whole being changed, and problems began. He would accuse my mother of having someone in the house and lash out at her like a high-level boxer, for no reason, when he came home drunk at night.

My mother and father met

My mother was a beautiful, submissive young woman with a radiant smile, raised on the outskirts of her city. She had a hardworking and cheerful mother and a father who liked to drink. Her father was also a womanizer and verbal abuser; he did not allow my mother to engage in any kind of relationship with men after she was an adult.

My dad used to travel for business and passed in front of the house where my mother lived with her parents almost every week in his beautiful "Green Lily" truck, as he called it.

My father was a very elegant, strong young man, and very persistent when he wanted something. He discovered my mother and began to pursue her. They met in secret because my mother's father was not very good with his children, and he was like my father: manipulative, a controller and probably would not allow her to have a romantic relationship. No man was good enough for my grandfather's daughter, according to my mother. My father was the first man in my mother's life and the only one she had. At the age of 19, she ran away with him to another place where my father lived. She left with her prince charming, not on a horse or in a carriage, but in the famous "Green Lily" truck.

Then she went to live somewhere else, a few hours away from her hometown. This handsome and charismatic young man promised my mother villas and castles, and she got courage and ran away with him, only to find out a few months later that he wasn't such a gentleman. She learned that he was already married and had five children with his wife. What? Are you amazed, dear reader? Yes, it was devastating for my mother.

Sadness, betrayal, and all those mixed feelings came over her. She was depressed and had many thoughts in her mind, as it is normal in a situation like that. She thought about leaving him, but I was already in her womb. She told me it was horrible for her; she saw herself against the wall. The arguments, the beatings, and the abuses of my father to her began. And now, what do I do? She asked herself. One day, she decided to leave him and go to my grandparents' house, only to find that there was a shortage of provisions at her parents' house. They were poor, and she also felt great indifference from her father and grandmother, who lived there, among many other struggles. Her father and grandmother were not very happy that she brought home another person who was already in her womb. That was "me". Hello, here I am, family! I would say from my mother's belly.

I was born with a midwife

A few months later, I was born in my great-grandmother's room, on her bed. In that same room, my great-grandmother had a spiritist altar. She was a midwife. My mother told me that I was born with the umbilical cord suffocating me. I turned blue, but I was already marked to be a warrior. I came out of that one unscathed and lived to tell you the story today, my reader.

Amid the precariousness in my grandparents' house, the negative attitude of her father and other conditions, she was able to stay there for only a few months. Prince Charming (my father) came to her rescue and convinced her to come back to him, telling her all the big promises she wanted to hear. Something like: That he was not living with his legal wife; that he loved my mother, and that one day he was going to solve that problem (by divorcing the other woman). My father cried, begged and put on a great show.

This is the character of the abusive man; he is manipulative and abusive. Violence and abuse are cycles.

My mother would return with him, and a few days later, after the honeymoon, the same hostile situation would begin again! She had one pregnancy after another, adding to and increasing the members of the family.

My father also kept the fire burning with his legal wife, because she became pregnant a few years after I was born. At the beginning of her relationship with my father, my mother had a son every two years, and after her first four daughters, she had a son or daughter every year until she reached a total of eleven. As we grew older, some of us helped my mother to be fixed, so that she would not have any more children; otherwise, who knows how many more she would have had, or died in childbirth? She was very frail, and the last child, the eleventh, was born small and very weak.

My mother's sad despair

In the early years of her relationship with my father, my mother tried many times to leave home and go to her parents or relatives and live with them or go somewhere far from my father, but her family could not support her economically or emotionally. They were hardworking people, but with low incomes. A few days after being at her family's house, she had to leave and return to her insistent partner, who always begged her to return to him, making her many promises of a better life, and that he would change and treat her better, and all that drama.

This is what my childhood was like. Seeing my mother being beaten, most of the time, she was crying, insecure, shy, and sad. We were overwhelmed at home because we didn't know what emotional state my father would be in when he came home next time. I panicked every time I saw him coming home. Sometimes my father would drive past the house on his motorcycle or his truck when he went to spend the night with one of his other women. When I used to see him passing by, I would run to visit our neighbours' house in the late afternoon or evening to watch TV at their house, but alertness and anxiety were in my heart. I was always aware and feared that my father might change his mind and come home, and I knew that we were at our neighbour's house. The nights he decided to stay with my mother were nights of fear and sadness for me. We walked as if on glass or eggshells with fear of everything. I didn't know how to act or what to expect. We went to bed early, whispering to each other, without speaking loudly, fearing that any step, or action of ours or our mother's would ignite the fire of the violent monster within my father. Like a monster, that's how I saw it and perceived it at that age.

As the firstborn, I helped with the care of my siblings, especially while my mother was pregnant, doing everything else with her big belly. I rocked my siblings in one of the pink rocking chairs we had in the living room and helped them sleep. I did housework to help my mother, went grocery shopping, cooked at a very young age, and more. I remember climbing on the bottom of a large empty can of cooking oil, so I could get to the old wood stove we had.

I used to have mixed feelings, pain, confusion, and even resentment when my mother, after being beaten so hard, would go to my grandparents' house; and then my father would seek her out, beg her, and convince her to come back to him, and she would reconcile with him repeatedly. When we were going back to our house after my father beat my mother, I had a lot of questions in my mind, and I was angry inside. I knew there would be a little honeymoon, another pregnancy, and again blows, fights, fears, heartaches, and scarcity in the house. We would return to our horrible normality. I always wondered: "Could it be that my mother likes to be mistreated and beaten?" Why does she go back to him all the time?

I didn't understand what I know today about abuse, domestic violence, manipulation, mental and emotional problems, and the codependency that comes from being abused. My mother depended on my father for everything, and as she didn't get help from her family, my father was the one who governed.

Partying with Dad

My father regularly had long parties at the house of one of his wives, or the house of a close friend or his family. Most of my father's siblings and friends loved to have parties, or what we call parranda in Spanish. I used to see my dad drinking and talking to his friends, eating sancocho (a meat and vegetable stew, typical of the Dominican Republic), an asopao or a locrio. They usually drank until dawn and sometimes for days.

Once, I went with my father to the house of one of his women, with whom he had two lovely children younger than me; she lived and still lives about 15 minutes from my mother's house. That night, everything was fine; he took me to the meeting with his friends at that house; she cooked for my father and his friends, and she also took good care of me, a very nice lady. My father drank, talked about everything with his bunch, made jokes, and laughed. I was very sleepy and just wanted to go home, but who could say anything to my father? Later, the party ended. Early morning, the next day, my father took me back home. I went to bed during the day, and a few hours later, I got up. My mother sent me to the grocery store to buy something for dinner. In front of the grocery store, one of my friends and schoolmates used to live. Here, I will refer to her as Cindy to protect her identity. She was about my age, about twelve or thirteen years old. When she saw me, she called me: "Joselyn, Joselyn!", and I went to greet her, but at that very moment, my father passed by on his motorcycle; he didn't stop to say anything, but he glanced at me. One of those looks that says that a great danger is coming. I panicked, quickly said goodbye to Cindy, went to the store across the street to buy what I had come to get, and went home.

When I walked in, I knew something was very wrong. My father was at home, and he seemed to be waiting for me. He looked furious. I arrived with the errands; I left them in the kitchen, and he called me and asked me: What were you doing talking to that prostitute? For some reason, or because of disputes between her father and him, my father despised her; I never knew why. Without having done anything wrong to my dad or me, he just hated her. I replied tremblingly, "I was greeting Cindy, she called me to say hello when I was going to the grocery store." I immediately saw something hellish, like hatred in his eyes. I said to him, trembling even more, "Forgive me, forgive me, Dad," as if I had done something unforgivable or very bad. I thought those words would soften him, but, on the contrary, they inflamed him more, as if instigated by an evil spirit. He immediately grabbed my arm and hit me with a yellow nylon lasso that was used with cows in the field at that time. That was one of the biggest beatings I suffered at the hands of my father. I fell emotionally into a very dark hole and place.

Do you remember my reader, that I had just accompanied him to his party with his friends the night before, and everything was merry and happy while they were drinking? The next day, this beating took place just because I was greeting a friend in front of her house for a few minutes. It's as if something evil was instigating my father. This sounds like a horror movie, but that was my reality.

I was so confused and hurt inside. Because one moment I saw my dad being kind, laughing and having fun with his friends, and the next, for no further reason, I saw a monster, an evil executioner in front of me screaming, scolding me, cursing me, and beating me like a mentally deranged man. With the lashes of the nylon loop, I could feel the urine and the number two coming out of my terrified and trembling little body. It was also the only time my mom overcame her fears and walked out of the kitchen where she was when she heard the cries of despair from me, saying, "Dad, forgive me, forgive me, Dad, I won't do it again."

When she saw me and saw that he was beating me with such force and anger, my mother screamed: "Are you going to kill her? Leave her alone!!" and added a few swear words. For the first time, I heard my mother swear at my dad amid her pain when she saw me beaten and lying in the dirt yard and bleeding. In my childhood, I honestly used to think that by the time I was an adult, my body would be like jelly from so many beatings and beatings that I endured week after week. In my little mind, I harboured that restlessness. I said to myself inside: "I think that when I grow up, like in my thirties, if I get there, my flesh will be very limp from all the blows I get." But now I'm here to tell my story, I'm grateful.

I thought my father hated me

In my mind, I could never understand it, and I thought my father hated me. Other people said that he expressed himself with fatherly love very often when he told them about me. I never heard him say anything sweet to me. I never heard him or my mother say I love you, you are important to me, I believe in you, anything like that. I don't remember him ever hugging me, nor did my mother.

How important it is to express words of love and affirmation to our children. If you are a father, mother, sibling, or family member, tell your children and your family, "I love you", "I believe in you", or "You are important to me" with positive words.

How important it is to know that our words edify or mark us for defeat.

I know that my parents were abused and mistreated in their childhood; they did not receive much love or affirmation from their parents. At that time, I did not know or understand these things.

This cycle must be broken intentionally. It can be achieved with faith and determination

I remember sneaking out to school for extracurricular and celebratory activities. I'm musical, I like to socialize, and I love people. If I participated in any activity in my school or community, it was in secret, because my dad might not have liked the idea. There was so much fear that I didn't even think about asking permission to tell you the truth. Maybe it could have been different, but the fear was so great that I decided not to. One day, my history teacher asked me to participate in an activity we called *Poetry Chore,* but knowing what I was dealing with at home, I asked her, "Teacher, could you write me a note to give to my dad? He is a bit complicated." The teacher (Mrs. Francisca) gladly wrote a quick note to my father and gave it to me. In the note, she expressed her desire for me to attend and be part of the school activity and participate. Doña Francisca did not have very nice handwriting, despite being a teacher, but I was at peace because the teacher helped me address my father. I thought everything was going to be fine with my father because it came from my teacher.

When I handed the note to my father, I saw that his face changed to an incredibly angry expression. He told me, "I would like to know the *Cuero* (*prostitute*), who did this with you to beat up the two of you, and you are going to remember for the rest of your lives." He also called me by some other not-very-nice names, which I won't write here.

I tried to explain it to him, but he thought a friend of mine or a classmate, or someone else, not the teacher, had written the note. I was not bitten on this specific occasion, but I was on the verge of it. For a moment, I thought I had earned one, but this time he didn't hit me. My father not believing in me; his negativity and distrust hurt me a lot in my heart. I was marked in life negatively in a terrific way.

I was smart and dreamed of being someone when I grew up to help my mother. I had talent, and I loved to sing. First, I wanted to be a singer; after all, I had an uncle, Andrés de Jesús, my mother's brother, who is a Master of Music and a professional arranger. He is well-known and good in his area. But my dad used to say to me that singers end up being prostitutes.

Then I dreamed of being a nurse, and my father discouraged me by saying that all nurses end up sleeping with the doctors. On several occasions, I heard my father say to my mother, "These daughters of yours will all be prostitutes," just to annoy her.

In the end, my mother had no voice or vote to make any decision about us; the one we had to ask for permission for everything, if we were brave enough, was my father; he was never happy with anything, and most of the time when he attacked and yelled at my mother and would break up with me, or start with me and end with my mother. I could never explain to myself what led him to be like that with us. I lived in an environment of fear, discouragement, and anger.

My mother was very submissive and passive. She never rebelled against my father or showed resistance to him, except for the day my father almost killed me, which I mentioned earlier. What my mother always used to say was that men are not good; they only make women suffer. She spoke from her wounds. This is how my childhood and early adolescence passed. I developed rebellion. I started sneaking out the windows at night to date older men. My attitude was that of a girl much older than my age. I was very angry. It was unbearable to see my mother suffer and be the victim of so many beatings and violence at the hands of my father.

He was a verbal and physical abuser. I also received the same treatment. We were defenceless, and I had it harder, especially because I was the oldest. I have so many painful stories from my childhood that I would need a few books to record them all, but I will mention the next story because it is relevant to what happened next.

A big problem

Josefina, a friend from school, asked me one day if she could come to my home and spend some time at my house on the weekend. I consulted with my mother, and she accepted. My mother and I were already exhausted, emotionally and mentally, from my father's actions. No one visited our house, not friends from school, not teachers, not anyone else, unless they were sneaking in. My father didn't want us to have friends or visit other houses. He was always suspicious, and everything bothered him. But yes, he could have friends, drinks, parties, and have many mistresses, as we call them in DR. My mother also didn't go out, except occasionally with him, and she didn't even enjoy it, as she was very shy and was also afraid of him.

Going back to my friend Josefina and her visit to my house, she wanted to go on Sunday, and as I said, I had reluctantly received my mother's approval, despite her concern that my father would find out. What I didn't know was that my friend had a boyfriend, and they agreed to meet at my house, because her mother didn't know anything about their relationship, and she couldn't go out with him from her home. After arriving at my house, Josefina explained the situation to me and later asked me to accompany her and her boyfriend to a place near my house that was a rural nightclub. Well, I was totally all for it, scared and all, I was fed up with my father. I went with them to the nightclub in a sector called Guanábano near my house.

When we arrived, they sat down at one table, put me at another, and left me alone. I could see them kissing and cuddling at the next table. They asked the waiter to serve me beers (yes, beers, in some places, they don't necessarily follow the law of not serving alcohol to minors). I started drinking beers like crazy, then it was rum, and I ended up drunk to the core.

When I got home late at night, my mother was furious. I had never seen her like this. I imagine she was worried that my father would come or pass by our house and not find me, or something, that's probably what made her so angry with me. I don't remember how I got home, nor where Josefina and her boyfriend were. I found myself at home, vomiting as if it were flames of fire from my mouth, like a dragon in the morning. I was very dizzy, and then I went to sleep.

In those rural communities and the countryside, we were surrounded by many of my father's snitches and friends, and he had many, I tell you. Everybody was in everyone's business, so my father soon found out about my drunkenness and my going out. My father never sat with me or my mother, nor did he ask if what people told him was true or not. He would just come and lash out at me or us, without even knowing if what he had been told was true. On many occasions, I felt or believed that my father hated me, but, on the other hand, I felt very good when he invited me to share in his parties with his friends and sometimes with some of my other brothers and sisters. It made me feel important to him, even if I just had to sit and listen to all his drunken conversations. I longed for his love and acceptance.

He kicked me out of his house at 13

Like I said, my dad found out that I went to the disco with my friend and got drunk. He kicked me out of the house at the age of thirteen. He came to the house with a *colin* (machete) in his hands and brought me an empty rum box, he said, "Joselyn, look at this box, take all your belongings, and leave my house! I'm going to be back in two hours, and if I find you in this house, I'm going to kill you!" This time, my mother and I understood it was a radical decision. Knowing my father, I knew that if he came back and found me in the house, the very least I would have would be a big beating that would leave me paralyzed or something like that. That was my expectation. I was full of fear. I think my mother was tired of seeing my father beating me until I did numbers one and two in the middle of the beating and heard my screams all over the house. My mother saw me many times, fearful of the beatings and whippings. He left us both with bruises.

I am marked in different parts of my body, on my skull, with a mark that will never grow hair. One day, my dad pulled my hair so hard after I had a chemical procedure, and I came home with my hair freshly straightened. I was only twelve years old; he dragged me all over the house, and that part of my skull got infected on my head, and all my hair was uprooted from that part of my head; hair will never grow there again. My father mistreated my mother and me; he vented his anger against us, and he was very domineering, especially with me and my dear mother. Something about him was toxic and demonic at the time. I endeavoured to please him; I wanted his approval (*all children want approval*), but the more I tried, the less it worked for me.

I was tired of living with so much fear, not knowing what his next reaction would be. If he arrived drunk or in a very bad mood, he would lash out at my mother or me. Who knew what he would do next?

I had developed an internal rebellion seeing a disciplinary, angry, and macho man do the opposite of what he demanded of me. Like, for example, having women wherever and whenever they wanted. He would disappear for days and leave us with no money and little or nothing to eat in the house, and then he would come back as if nothing had happened, he would park in front of our small house with another woman, he would leave her inside the truck, he would enter the house, he would not even talk to my mother or us, he would leave us two or three pesos for food and leave again as if everything was fine and normal. I was tired of seeing my mother say nothing when things like that happened, but the pale, sad expression on her face that showed anguish and pain was more than I could bear. The day my father kicked me out, my mother, hearing what he said, advised me to go to my grandmother's house. I put what I could in the rum box as fast as I could, and then stood in front of my poor, lethargic little house waiting for transportation to go to my grandmother's house. I was afraid and uncertain of what the future was going to be. All kinds of thoughts came into my mind.

Many memories, tears, the pain of leaving my mother and my siblings, what I loved most, and sad to see my mother sobbing. But deep down, free from that sentence on my life. "At least I'll be out of my father's reach and control," I thought.

Even though I had an uncertain future, there was a pleasant feeling of being free and getting out of my life's terrifying yoke. My first executioner would be left behind. As fast as I could, I stopped a transportation car and headed to the city, then two more cars, to get to my grandmother's house.

Previously, when my mother left my father after a fight and a big beating and went to my grandmother Flora's house, I always wanted to stay with my grandmother and not go back to my parents' house. I enjoyed being with my grandmother; she was sweet, and I felt loved and welcomed by her. We communicated well and had conversations about different things. We used to go out to visit her family and friends and enjoy walking together as if she were my mother. She was beautiful and in good physical shape; she always dressed well and looked good. She was a dressmaker and a very hardworking woman. I was born in her house. She lived with her husband and her mother-in-law, the midwife. She used to have me during my early years. I desperately wanted to stay at her house. Before my mother and my father were back together after a big fight, it was a show, with a lot of drama, with my father crying and asking for forgiveness; it was the same thing repeatedly. My mother refused to forgive him for a few hours, and then, she used to look for many justifications why she should go back with him; like the children, the economic situation, his family, my father's promises, and so on. Finally, she convinced herself to return with him. My father always went to look for her with his friends. He would bring food and gifts to my grandparents' house, get drunk and insist on asking my mother for forgiveness. She refused to listen to him or sit with him in the first hours of the visit, but as time went by, my mother was already softening until she agreed to return to him. He used to say: "Elida, forgive me, I won't do it again, I'll change, I love you." And he began to cry like a baby. The same thing was repeated for hours. It was so pathetic. Oh, for me, it was so irritating and frustrating. When my mother reconciled with my father and was ready to go back to him, I used to throw a tantrum and cry like crazy because I didn't want to go with them. My grandmother was so sweet and good to me.

But now, as a teenager, my father had kicked me out of his house. I left my parents' house with my grandparents in other conditions. I would live forever with my grandmother, I thought. At least I got out of the torture and pain of seeing my mother suffering, and all the violence inflicted on my body as well. I arrived in the city of Castillo and then headed to Yaiba, a rural area on the outskirts of that city in the Dominican Republic, where my grandmother lived. I arrived at my grandmother's house, which was blue and redwood, which had many pansy bushes of all colours in the front, and behind the house, they had many large coconut trees, shrubs, almonds and cashews, among other pretty fruits and flowers. My great-grandmother (my grandfather's mother) kept the yard beautiful; she used to cut the grass and weeds with a machete, and it always looked beautiful.

On my arrival, my grandmother received me as always, with much love. She liked to have me in her house and always wanted me to stay and live with her, but my father had never accepted it. Now I was there forever, at least that was what I thought.

Chapter 2
Sexually Raped

At my grandmother's house, I started to go out by myself. It was good to be free. I became interested in men older than me. One family friend began to flirt with me, and well, that made me feel good and important. I was only 13 years old. That was going on for a few months. I let him flirt with me, and I did the same with him as well, but a few weeks later, I found out that he had a partner, and they had some kids. One afternoon, this man passed by my house trying to chat with me, and I complained and was very upset because he had not told me about his partner and his children. He passionately and regretfully told me the same story that most men do in these cases: He told me, "We are not married, I don't love her, we sleep in separate beds, all those lies."

That afternoon, we argued a lot, and I ended the friendship. At the end of our conversation, when I thought he had understood and would leave me alone, my cousin, who was living at the time at my grandparents' house with me, asked him to take her to town to buy some soda and cake that we needed for a birthday of a friend who lived nearby in the area. It was her birthday that day. This man and I were standing in front of each other, we were still arguing, when my cousin approached us, and we were looking at each other as if to say: What do we do now? My cousin didn't know what was going on; she didn't even know that we liked each other, or that we had a little secret romance. She asked him to go with us as she didn't want to go alone, plus she needed a ride. I hesitated to go. But I did not want her to suspect what was going on between me and that man. I agreed to go with her.

Deep down, I was hurt by my suitor's lies. He agreed to take us to the grocery store, and we got into his truck to go to town. He was driving, and I was in the middle, with my cousin next to me on the right. When we arrived at the store at the city entrance, my cousin said, "I'll be right back. Will you come in with me?" I wasn't in the mood to go shopping or anything like that. I said no, I'll wait for you here inside the vehicle. It was already dark, and I thought it would only take my cousin a few minutes to do what she needed to do. I stayed in the vehicle, waiting for her. The least that crossed my mind was what happened next. This man and I began to argue again because he wanted me to believe his story, and he tried to convince me of his truth again. He did not give up on what we had previously discussed. Suddenly, with the right door not fully closed, this man began to drive in the middle of the town with me inside. It was already dark; my cousin was still inside the store buying what she came for, and this man, like a madman, accelerated angrily down the street. I was in shock, trying to make him stop and come back. I started yelling at him: "Where are you going? Return! What are you doing?" I was shouting at him, but he was furious and drove with me in the middle of the street in that small town. The streets were lonely; people were in their homes at nightfall. I tried to jump out of the truck when I feared that he was planning something bad, maybe to kill me, because he was speeding wildly. My right door wasn't locked. I thought about jumping, but I was terrified of jumping onto the sidewalk and street pavement. My heart was pounding; my hands were cold, and I looked around to see if I could find someone to shout to from the moving truck, but there was no one in sight.

This enraged man crossed the small town of Castillo at a terrifying speed, drove the truck out of the city and climbed a hill between cocoa plantations that are very typical of the area. He knew the area very well, as his father owned cocoa plantations and sold the product wholesale. His father was a rich man, and all his children worked with him. At one point,

I found myself in immense darkness, without a single soul around us, we were surrounded by many trees, shrubs and leaves on the ground, and no visible houses. I never knew, but maybe that property was also owned by his family. He stopped suddenly, and I jumped out of that truck and ran through all that darkness with all my might. My beautiful sandals flew off my feet, I ran and ran like a roadrunner, I was short of breath, scared, the guy was chasing me, I hoped I could find a way out in the middle of such dense darkness, the man behind me was running faster, I realized the bad intention of my pursuer who was tall and strong. At one point, running around without even knowing where I was, out of breath and panicking, I lost my strength and fell. I was caught by my pursuer. I felt that monster on top of me, tearing my clothes, and panting, I had no strength to resist anymore. The next thing for me was pain, blood, tears, fear for my life, and hearing this man crying, saying: "I want you for myself and you are mine, I will marry you, I will take care of you," and so much more nonsense. Phew! This sounds like a horror movie or something like that, but it's my story, the one I can tell now without pain, but which was so disgusting, painful, and embarrassing before.

Coming back to the scene at the time, I just wanted to get out of that jungle and horrific place and be in a safe. I didn't know how to get out of there, so I needed to pretend that I was calm and somehow agreed with what he was saying, so that he would take me back. I was very afraid for my life. I didn't know what this maniac would do next. After that, the rapist didn't stop talking trying to fix the situation with me in a way that was good for him. We spent hours going round and round, I had all kinds of mixed feelings and a lot of physical and emotional pain. I didn't know what to do, at that moment I was helpless and thought: How am I going to face my grandmother? What am I going to do? Should I tell her? No, I thought it was better if I did not, because that would make the situation worse and so on. My cousin was at the party for a few hours, and she was anxious and worried, wondering where I was. I asked the perpetrator to take me back to where my cousin was. I was now in a very dark place emotionally again, not knowing what to say and what would be next in my life. This man left me in front of the house where my cousin was. He told me not to talk and promised me that he would fix everything. My cousin didn't want to leave the party without knowing where I was. It was around 9 or 10 at night, which was late in that part of the world at that time. Nor did she dare to come to my grandmother's house without me. At that time, there were no telephones or communication like today.

I decided to clean myself as best I could; luckily, my dress was dark, and the blood stain of my virginity was not noticeable, and it was also night. I didn't know what to do. That man asked me not to tell my family until I decided to marry him. I was very anxious, angry, and afraid. He left me at the entrance of the house, where my cousin was waiting for me, along with some people who were still present at the party. My cousin saw me coming, jumped out of her chair and asked me, "Where have you been?!!" She said other words not very pleasant to me, angrily. "Where did you go? What were you doing? Are you crazy? If I go home without you, I could be in trouble!" She yelled at me and yelled at me. I decided not to speak, I was exhausted, but now I was more afraid than when I ran in the middle of those dark cocoa trees and heard the voice of my persecutor. I told my cousin about it, and she was scared. I didn't know whether to hit or hide, or what to do. I asked her not to say anything to my grandmother. We were in trouble.

I didn't know what to do, but something had been ripped from my life, something very important, and here I was practically alone, keeping this secret from my grandmother, the only one I had on my side. I had so much confusion in my life, even more so at the time, because of what was happening. I don't know what the next step would be, but I knew that, despite my age, fourteen already, I thought I knew everything, but I was like a kitten inside, without solution, with pain, shame, confusion, and condemnation. I felt that it was my fault for provoking that man's anger, or for telling him that we will no longer be friends, or for taking a ride with him, instead of staying at home. I should not have spoken to him negatively, I am not good, oh God, I have so much shame and pain. Now I have more pain, frustration and added rebellion. Anyway, my cousin and I went to my grandparents' house, and they were already asleep. We went to bed; my cousin didn't ask any more questions, and I didn't want to talk. A day passed, and another day passed. On the third day, I couldn't take it anymore, so I told my grandmother the best I could.

"Oh, Father, don't tell me, and now, what are we going to do?" These were the words of my grandmother. My grandmother was worried about me, but she was confused, frustrated, and angry; they never thought that this close friend could do this. She took me to a doctor to be examined immediately and confirm that I had recently been raped. My grandmother was very anxious and worried, too, I imagine meeting my father. I think she was in a very difficult situation. I was still a minor, and my father had rights over me. How would my father react? would he blame her?

My grandmother told my grandfather about the case. He did not show much interest or concern. I imagine it was nothing to him, after all, my grandmother ran away with him when she was thirteen, and until that day, she had been his wife and the mother of his children. But my grandmother went further in her way of wanting to help me. She went to visit my father in Moca and told him what had happened, risking being mistreated with words or that my father would say something offensive to her or something like that. I guess she was looking for help to find a solution to this situation. She came from visiting my dad, extremely disappointed because my dad had no interest in helping me or doing anything for me. My father just listened to the information and told her to do whatever she wanted. My father showed no interest in agreeing with her to bring the one who had raped her daughter to justice or to support me. My grandmother, my dear Flora, a fighter, diligent and kind-hearted woman, went further and went to court to denounce the aggressor. To this day I think that the medicine (the process of going to court) was as painful as the disease, (the rape); In other words, her solution affected me greatly, but I also recognized my grandmother's desire to help me. She was hurt by what had happened to her beloved granddaughter, and as she said at the time, "I want that man to give you back your dignity." I didn't understand it, but I appreciated her effort and love for me. The only thing I had in life was my sweet grandmother Flora.

In a court

I was registered in the legal system. The accused was notified. In those days, the procedure for rape was not as strict as it is today, at least in my country. Abuse, domestic violence and rape were something that was dealt with between families. Most of the time, depending on the system and society, the woman was blamed, whether she was a girl or an adult woman. We are a society that still has a lot of machismo and violence from both sexes. My grandmother had no money, we had to apply for a free lawyer to the courts, and his family sought out an expensive lawyer.

In front of a judge

I wanted the floor to swallow me, standing the first time of so many times in front of a judge, with a court full of people. Some of those people were there with their different cases to deal with that day, others curious, lawyers, and their assistants waiting to present their different cases. Among those cases was mine. There I was dealing with my emotions, my heart pounding with fear, shame and worries about what they will say, not knowing what to expect, my knees shaking and very weak, overwhelmed. In those days, virginity was the most sacred thing a young woman possessed. In my culture, when one lost that virtue, without having a husband or partner, that young woman was not worth much. They referred to us victims with expressions such as "she is not good".

People were starting to look at us littler crazy ones, good for nothing, than young women who needed help, protection, and support. So, the news running everywhere. In small towns the news spreads like wildfire, and everyone finds out everything and wants to know everything about everyone. On top of that, having to appear in court so often, repeatedly saying what had happened to me, was very tedious. There were endless interrogations and periodically going in front of a judge to listen to the prosecutor's questioning and indirect words of accusation, it was very uncomfortable, irritating and painful for me. The prosecutor said something like this: "With the reputation that these young women have today, I am sure that this young woman provoked him." "You know, Your Honor, that these days this young generation of girls is provoking men, especially when they know that the man has money," and many other things of the sort. My emotions, what I was feeling and the terrifying embarrassment of being there in front of so many people hearing all this were unbearable, I don't think anyone cared much about me back them, except for my dear grandmother.

In the early days of the case, my lawyer was very enthusiastic, apparently upset with the perpetrator, he advised us on what to do, but in my culture, money could buy and influence a lot , at least back then. Money helped corrupt people and crooked system money change their minds. Weeks and months passed. I don't remember the time, one trip after another to the Judicial Court, but nothing was resolved; having to go to court hurt me internally every time I went. Within a few months, my lawyer suddenly lost interest in the case, the court postponed the case many times. In our country, it was customary to drag out the matter in court so that the cases are weakened, and, at the end, people give up, withdraw the accusation or reach an agreement.

This man's family was wealthy and influential in that sector. The man said in court: “I will marry her.” I was told that in those days, when a man raped a girl and afterwards said "I'm marrying her" the Department of Justice couldn't do anything to him. I don't know if that's true, at least that's what I understood when someone told me. One day the lawyer came to visit us to tell me that the case was very difficult because the offender offered me a home and wanted to get married, and other legal departments thought it would be better to let the case be dealt with between us. Everything was resolved in court without my grandmother and I being present. I didn't want to know anything about all this anymore. The man kept looking for me and appearing to me everywhere I went. Every night, at least during the case duration, he went with loudspeakers in front of my grandmother's house to play music of love with his friends. I don't know what he wanted to prove.

I was demoralized, but life had to go on. Now more pain, trauma and a greater rebellion within me, deep insecurities and rejection. I always lived on the defensive side, and with a lot of pain and sadness. I couldn't understand why I had to go through so much since I was a child. I didn't understand why some people who were supposed to love me hadn't shown any interest in me, except for my grandmother. I never heard the words “I love you, you are important to me, I am proud of you, I believe in you.” No words of encouragement or affirmation. As far as I can remember, no one hugged me, and I never had an expression of love in my parental home or anywhere else. I was a victim of my circumstances.

Reader, you already know what my father was like, and my mother was a shy and submissive woman. She was terrified of my father, and her feelings and emotions were transmitted to her children. I lived with such fear and agony that it produced terrible insecurity in my life, I had suicidal thoughts, especially after the rape.

The rape was terrible, it deepened the rejection within me, and it increased the rebellion that I already carried inside. I lost respect for men, I started dating men for what they gave me and for fun to , but inside me there was a deep need and an emptiness.

I used to leave my grandparents' house at night without them noticing or giving me their consent, as I used to do at my parents' house. My grandmother found out and the fights with her began. My father gave me shots of alcohol when I was a child, and I got drunk very bad the day of my friend date. Now I was drinking seriously and didn't want to listen to my dear grandmother.

When I turned 15 at my grandmother's house, I was already an adult woman in my mind. I thought I wasn't going to be intimidated by any man or trampled down by anyone.

I went to visit my mother a couple of times. I was sneaking into her house, because I missed her, but I didn't want to have anything to do with my dad, and I didn't know what he would do if he knew I was at home, so I had to visit my mother secretly.

My grandmother was going crazy about what had become her favourite girl. She was so desperate to help me that she even took me to a witch. This witch began to do very strange rituals on me. I had to go to consult her weekly, give me some bathing rituals, light candles, say some prayers, etc. Although at first, I didn't understand what was going on, nor did I understand the whole thing about witchcraft, I became dependent on going to the witch, consulting her, and believing that all of that would improve my life, but of course, we always had to pay the witch good money.

That is a mistake of the family to introduce their children or relatives to witches and expose them to the occult at a young age or at any time, what that adds is curses and covenant with darkness, and eventually misfortune, evil and poverty. The Lord hates idolatry and divination. Because there is only one God, and we are only to serve and worship Him and depend on Him alone.

Back then I thought, well, nobody cares about me, I'm going to do my best to be myself and I don't care about anything or anyone else. I was already a woman, I slept with those I wanted to sleep with, I used them and let them use me. Without a job, without finishing school, they were intense years and months. I was a teenager, but in my head, I was an adult, according to me, I knew it all. When I was fifteen , I met a man much older than me, with whom I got involved in a love relationship. I knew part of his family who lived in the same community just a few minutes from my grandmother's house. He lived in the big city, the capital of the Dominican Republic, and travelled to that part of the country where his family and my grandmother lived. Quickly we started a relationship, and he asked me to go to live with him in the capital which was a few hours away, and I accepted.

I wanted so bad to run away from that place where I used to live, at least I would be out of sight of those people who knew me, pointed, and criticized me. I needed a change of place and people.

Chapter 3
Capital, here I come!

I left my grandparents' home. They knew I was going with this man and there was nothing they could do. I was stubborn and I didn't listen to any of their advice. He was 15 years older; I consented to go with him. This man picked me up and took me to the capital city. We arrived at his parents' home. His relatives were very close to each other, very good and decent people, they received me well. My partner built a small room attached on the back of his parents' house and we lived there for a period of less than a year. What I didn't know was that the man before knowing me had a girlfriend. He was in a long-term relationship with a commitment to get married. He left this girlfriend in one fell swoop for me. His parents weren't happy about it. The fights and disagreements began, jealousy on both sides on the part of him and me, blows, shouting of bad words and abuse.

Here is something to ponder: *Abused women or men attract those of their kind. It's a vicious cycle until that circle is broken . It can be broken with determination and faith, accepting that we need help and receiving it. But the women or men need to do their part despite how their feel. They can get out of that cycle.*

Now I was experiencing the same situation that occurred between my parents. I became pregnant by this man, three months after I arrived in the capital. Now, what should I do? I asked myself. I knew deep down that this relationship wouldn't work. I had found my father in this man, and even worse, because with him I had to go to bed whether I wanted to or not.

I began to look for an alternative as to how I could get out of that relationship and where I could live. He used to hit me hard; we used to fight for real. At that time I was also violent. We mistreated each other. I couldn't bear to feel like a prisoner in his parents' house. But I had little strength, I was a young girl 16 years old, against a big, tall man. In my parents' house at least I had some freedom when my father was away, but now I was under the permanent surveillance of my abuser and when he was not at home, his family was watching. That was how I perceived it.

I'm going to take my own life

There was a time when I didn't want to live anymore. I dedicated myself to planning how I was going to commit suicide. In my parents' home at least I had some freedom when my father was away, but now I was under the permanent surveillance. One day, after a big fight, I decided that I was going to drink a lot of alcohol and then, I would drink a hair dye. I don't know where the idea of taking hair dye came from. I don't know if I heard it from someone, or I didn't want to die, perhaps that's why I looked for the least toxic chemical, I do not know. I went to a small grocery store. In my home country, we call a business that sells food and beverages at retail a "colmado." I sat down and drank a few brugalitas, (a small bottle of rum typical of my country), until I got drunk. When I was drunk, I went behind the grocery store, opened the dye, and drank it. The owner of the grocery store appeared on the scene and immediately called the ambulance, and my partner's family, they knew each other, and the house was nearby. Suddenly I found myself in an ambulance being rushed to the hospital and the father of my child near me, he was very angry and panicking, wondering if I was crazy, and wondering why I had done such a thing. The nurses and doctor met me at the door of the hospital and rushed me from the ambulance at full speed to the emergency room. They put tubes in my stomach, and the cleaning began. I am thankful that my child was not harmed. Oh my God, how crazy I have been! After the hospital, I returned to my partner home. Then we moved to a small place that my partner rented. We moved in what we call our home. It was in one of the poorest and most crime-ridden neighborhoods in my country then, *Las Cañitas*. We had a bed, a tabletop stove and a small dining set with four chairs, that was all. There was violence, criminal activity, and a lot of poverty around us.

My son was born

I gave birth to my first child in a public maternity hospital for low-income women, *La Altagracia Maternity Hospital.* My son was born healthy, weighted 9 and a half pounds. I almost died in childbirth; he was a very big, handsome boy and I was physically frail, a 16-year-old girl, skinny. In those days, public maternity hospitals did not have all the means we have today to care for pregnant women. In my case, the doctor said my case was for a cesarian section, but it was too late. At that moment, I had 2 doctors pressing the baby with their hands on the top of my belly, another using forceps to channel his head. My son was born cute, but with his head very long from the extreme force through the birth canal. It took me many days to recover from the labour and delivery.

Everything got worse

I had no way to be able to work. I had a small baby, with no training, no experience. I did not have anyone who could help me. My grandparents lived many hours away. It was just my partner and me. I was alone with him, with no family nearby. This increased the abuse of my aggressor, knowing that I was trapped and had no one to defend me. I received extreme beatings. The worst thing for me was the embarrassment of knowing that the whole neighbourhood was aware of our fights and the blows I received, but no one intervened. Everyone acted as if they didn't know or hear anything. The next day after a beating, everyone acted as if nothing had happened; they just looked at me with that little look of "we heard everything between you", those were my thoughts. Even seemed to me that some of them were laughing silently. In that neighbourhood, there were many shacks very close to each other, and everyone knew what was happening in almost every one of them. I tried to run several times, but where do I go next? I started planning where I could go and what I should do. One thing I knew, I couldn't go back with my son to my grandparents' house. They were poor and could not help me or my son. I didn't think about going back to my parents' house either. My dad always said, "The day one of you leave this house, don't come back if you bring a child. " I didn't leave the house; he kicked me out, but I was already out of the house anyway. In addition, the father of my son threatened to hurt me if I dared to take our son and run away. It was horrible, but finally, one day, I built up the courage and left him. Someone helped me, and I was able to go to another house far from that neighbourhood. What mattered most to me was to leave him. I went to live in another dangerous and bad neighbourhood, in another part of the city, called *The Capatillo.*

Every Dominican knows where that neighbourhood is. But he found out where I was. He chased me everywhere. I was out of work with a son, with many needs and without many options. It was hell. I convinced myself that I couldn't do it alone and decided to accept him back into my life. A few days passed, and we were fine. Then the honeymoon ended, and the war began again. As always, I was very emotionally embarrassed by the messes we used to make and everything else that followed; lots of beatings and beatings, plus the shame of being cursed, and the screaming everywhere, while many listened and wondered what the hell was going on in my house.

Once this man hit me with a metal hanger that he had untied and formed a long wire and bent it in two. The reason for that specific beating was that I had started telling him that I didn't want to be with him anymore, and I didn't want to have sex with him. He left me with my body neatly cut, bleeding from the metal clothes' hanger he used to beat me. He was crazy. It was like he was demon-possessed. We argued and fought very badly, and he would turn into a monster when he wanted sex and was denied. Literally, that day he took me out of the house to the patio and hit me with many people around listening, and me crying from the depths and screaming very loudly and very scared. No one did anything to stop him and help me, or call, even if it was to call the police. I escaped to different places for days or months, wherever I could find a place to go with my son. He was always looking for me. He threatened, screaming and with rage. He chased me, claiming: "That is my son, and I have the right to see him and be with him." He said this repeatedly, but then, when he visited us, he wanted sex. I didn't know what to do. I felt like I was in a labyrinth with no way out. I didn't want to give up my son, but my son and I were now suffering, going through harsh times, and needed to survive.

A difficult and painful decision

He didn't know how to get me to bow to him. Some days he promised me the stars and the moon and bowed down saying that he loved me and would change; and other days he was furious and screamed and hit me with anything he found. So, this time, I didn't want anything to do with him, and I didn't give in to his new invitations to go out with him. My son was almost two years old. With a lot of pain in my soul, thinking about what was best for my son, I decided to give him to his father. After all, his father had a job and a salary, and he also had a family who loved him very much. I remember crying all night the day I gave away my son to his father.

My soul was torn apart for many days, but in the end, I think it was the best thing for the child and me. At that age, without anyone's support, where could I go? I had nothing to offer my son. In my country, we didn't have any support from the government for single mothers or children in need (I don't know if they do). As with domestic violence, it wasn't treated the way it is now. Almost nothing was done with the complaints of so many women abused by their partners, and many women have been found dead or mutilated. At the time I am writing, domestic violence and abuse treatment have improved, but we need much more help.

Domestic violence of both sexes in our nations and around the world needs more attention, more dedication, more intervention, more prevention, more support and help. Even though over time governments have become more aware and are giving much better support to battered women or domestic violence, the need remains great.

If you, or anyone you know, is reading this book and is being abused in any way, remember that there is always a way out, seek help, and God will have your back. You are important and valuable; you were not born to be abused or mistreated; you have the right to a dignified and peaceful life. Stand firm, make the decision. There is hope in that situation, even if everything seems dark now, you must get up and seek help. Receive this for yourself or to advise others.

Now, without my son, I went to live in a house where the owner rented rooms individually to single girls, and I started looking for a job. It was difficult, because in an underdeveloped country, for women without any education, experience, or training, without any relationship, you will most likely not find a place to work.

There I was living in a house with some other young women, finally felt free. This was another kind of freedom. But guess what? Once again, the father of my son found the place where I lived and came almost every day to ask me to go out with him. He said he loved me; he needed me and tried to persuade me back.

He almost killed me; I was on the verge of death

For the first time, I stood firm in my decision. I didn't want anything to do with him. I wouldn't sleep with him anymore! That specific afternoon, I was coming from the street, and he was waiting for me in front of the house. We started arguing right there in the front porch of the house. I was tired and opened the front door to get in. I thought that by persistently telling him no and discouraging him, he would finally leave. But he was asking me to go to a motel with him. I kept saying no, when suddenly this man again unleashed his fury; I saw the threats in his eyes, the violence and hatred. The other girls that I lived with were not yet in the house; they were working. The house had a long hallway with different rooms on one side of the house. He looked like he was coming from work; he had his military boots and pants, but a white T-shirt instead of his regular work shirt.

This time, he grabbed me desperately and furiously. I pulled away and ran to the room and locked myself in, but in that house, the rooms didn't reach the ceiling, and there was a gap between the ceiling and the walls of the rooms. The next thing I saw was this man climbing over the wall with his body in a riding position, preparing to jump into where I was. Immediately, when I sensed his intention to trap me inside the room and probably force me to have sex or to beat me, I opened the door, intending to run down the corridor and run away, but my pursuer, instead of jumping into my room, jumped to the other side, to the room where I was desperately trying to escape. When he saw me opening the door, he instantly grabbed me. Then he began to beat me and beat me with his fists with a malignant, diabolical rage, mixed with jealousy and impotence.

Today I understand that he was blinded by a diabolical force, full of anger, I know what was behind him, trying to cut off my life and my purpose, "Satan himself". The same spirit that had influenced my father to abuse and beat me also used my relationships to try to destroy me. That day, that man beat me so hard that I thought he was going to kill me. After he hit me so hard in the face with his fists, he took my right arm and began to twist it with all his strength and fury. He was a strong and muscular man. With so much pressure, my upper arm split in half. When that arm broke, I saw "little stars," and I fainted from the pain. I felt my arm fall dismembered and separated from my body. While I was on the ground, half dead, he took the other arm, the left arm and began to twist it; he also loosened it in half but did not break it. Then he lifted his right leg, with his strong military boots, to step on my face while I lay on my back on the floor in pain, half passed out, unable to move. But a neighbour who had been hearing it all came up, pushed the door open and shouted as loud as he could. "Are you going to kill her, son of... !" Then he suddenly stopped and left the house in a hurry. He crossed the street to take public transportation and headed to his mother's house on the other side of town. He said to his mother: "I killed Joselyn," then he went and turned himself in at the military base. My neighbours called the ambulance, took me to the nearest hospital, and put both of my arms in a cast. For 3 months, my face was unrecognizable, I could barely move, and everything hurt. A beautiful old lady, María Eugenia, my neighbour, bathed me and fed me. My family was notified, and my father came to visit me.

My father was angry and resentful of the man who had done this to his daughter; he was ready to press charges and make this man pay for his actions. He talked to every influencer he knew. He took a picture of me where I was unrecognizable; my dad was emotionally hurt over what happened. How ironic life is, isn't it? Until this incident, my father had not realized all the damage and pain he had also caused to other fathers' daughters, like my mother, or any of his other partners, in the same way. Now my father wanted this man to pay for what he had done to his daughter. How pathetic, hah?

At one time, one of this man's military superiors came to visit me and asked, "What do you want us to do with him?" Because he could be dishonourably discharged. But I knew that my son had no financial support from anyone else, and I could not meet his needs. I felt within me to respond to the commander: "I forgive him." I'm not going to press charges. I wasn't a Christian, but I felt like forgiving him. My dad never found out that I was the one who decided not to press charges. But he was furious with the system that had been unable to do anything for his daughter. I couldn't believe it. After that, the father of my son left me alone forever. He continued his way. He later married someone else, and today he has a good family. I want to clarify that today, he is a different person, a peaceful man. I must also say that my son grew up with him. Many years later, this man asked me to forgive him for all the abuse he had done to me. I had already forgiven him long before, so that I could move on. Today I also thank his wife for her help to my eldest son, they practically raised him. There are no bad feelings or evil between us at the time I write. As I said, I now realize who instigated my father and all the men who wanted to kill me: The enemy of our souls, Satan. Proof of this is that the person who almost killed me that day, many years ago, today is a man with a good, stable and peaceful family; he is a different man. Today, we maintain communication as two decent and peaceful people, our son is in the middle, and we love him.

My life went on. I wanted to be different and to be someone important in life, to be successful and have a stable life, but I didn't know what to do or where to go. I was looking for stability in men, doing things my way. I had no help or guidance, I had not finished high school, and I was living in a system based on using and letting others use me. At that time, my life went from one bad experience to another, always seeking security, peace and satisfaction. By the time I turned twenty, I had been through so much that I already felt like an old woman. What had changed was my relationship with my father.

At home, his relationship with my mother was going downhill. My siblings were growing up, and they didn't agree with seeing my father mistreat and beat her for anything. They were fed up with it. One day, my father was about to beat my mother, and my brothers defended our mother and confronted my father, and he left her alone from that day on.

At that time, I went from the capital to visit my mother, and when my father passed by the house, he greeted me. He was not violent with me, and we talked for a while. There were times when I looked at him with compassion because something was missing in his soul. I could sense it. But I was still afraid and unsure about talking to him, even for many years after I was an adult. Fear haunted me for most of my life. I was afraid of the authority figure. I was afraid of being alone, fear of what might happen tomorrow, a fear of rejection, and so many other fears.

Childhood traumas are for real; they must be treated, healed and released from our souls. They cannot be ignored or covered under the rug; they must be confronted, and help must be sought. There is healing available for trauma and pain.

Like I said, I always heard my mother say that men are not good, that they don't appreciate any woman, and that they are only good at mistreating women. Of course, she spoke from her wounds, and from all the bitterness she harboured in her heart, for the abuse she had suffered since her childhood. What I heard repeatedly stuck in my heart. Since I almost saw myself in the arms of death, I became more stubborn and independent, and none of the relationships I had were genuine or lasted long. So, I wanted to leave the country. I could not find a way to keep on with life on my own in my homeland. In my heart, there was always an inner plea, or a desperate cry for help, unconsciously, even if I was smiling. I sought help from witches, santería, warlocks, card readers, and sorcerers. I did all the rituals these people would recommend; lamps, prayers, candles, bath, perfume and so on, until I spent the little money I could get. On one occasion (this is a very funny story), I was in a new apartment that I had rented, and it almost burned down. I lit a candle behind the bedside table to Anaisa (an entity to attract and tie men supposedly), and the place caught fire. When I woke up, the flames almost reached me in bed. I can laugh now, but at the time, it was frustrating for me, because I was wondering: Why would someone who is my protector allow my house to be burned? Today, I know that all those wrong beliefs and practices bring curses, poverty, pain, darkness, and tragedies into our lives and even to our generations.

We are not to have idols, or practice witchcraft, or divination. They come from hell and bring us darkness and current, and generational curses.

You shall have no other gods before me. "You shall not make for yourself a carved image, or any likeness of anything that is in heaven above, or that is in the earth beneath, or that is in the water under the earth. You shall not bow down to them or serve them, for I, the Lord your God, am a jealous God, visiting the iniquity of the fathers on the children to the third and the fourth generation of those who hate me, but showing steadfast love to thousands of those who love me and keep my commandments. Exodus 20:3-6

Chapter 4

I am going to fly somewhere else!

I met a man named Delfin. He offered to take me to Puerto Rico, and I didn't hesitate to say yes. The only thing that allowed me to leave my country at that time was to get married immediately. So, we put everything together and got married. We had to wait a few months for my papers to arrive. He came to visit me a few times until I finally got my papers and went to Puerto Rico. The year was 1986.

When I arrived in Puerto Rico, he took me to his late wife's house, where one of his three children and his wife also lived. It was a very gloomy and antique house. He bought me a bed.

I tried to get used to my new life, new country, new customs, and even new food. Nothing was the same.

Well, that's when we started getting to know each other. Now, we were under the same roof, but how heavy it was for me. A few days after my arrival, I learned that this Puerto Rican man had lived for many years with a woman, and she was his partner for a long time, even before his previous wife passed away. He never told me about her. I found out later that this woman had come to my country when I was there, trying to find me, but she didn't see me. Delfin and I were already in a relationship. Who knows what she had in mind when she came to look for me? For me, he was a widower and was single.

A few weeks after I arrived in Puerto Rico, that woman was in a supermarket where I was buying some groceries; I didn't even know she existed at that time. Later, I learned that she was looking for me to kill me because she was angry and jealous, full of rage against me. I found out about it through Delfin's son, who told me about it later. I didn't even know that had happened. Once again, someone from above took care of me and prevented me from being harmed or killed, this time at the hands of an enemy I didn't know existed. But I watched as he went to work and came home late at night, he acted strangely and began to show signs of violence.

He was very harsh when I didn't agree to his wishes. We had great arguments, and he shouted like you wouldn't believe it. At times, I felt the devil in this man. As far as I knew, my long-time partner practiced witchcraft. People used to go to consult her; she was a medium and deeply involved in the occult. My partner’s son and his wife lived in the same house as us. They were members of a church. I observed that when they came home from church, they were delighted. I was invited a couple of times, but I always made excuses not to go. But a few weeks after I arrived, I thought, well, I must get rid of their persistent invitation to go to church. I'll go, and that'll be it. That's how I decided to go to church with them on a Sunday night. They liked to go at night because they slept during the day.

One night, when he wasn't home, I went to church. My soul became mournful because I was living with the same kind of abusive man as in my past relationships in my home country. I was a whirlwind of negative emotions, confusion, and sadness. I missed my country with everything I had. I went with them to the church, and when I arrived, it was full of people. They looked happy and greeted me with big smiles.

I saw them praising and raising their hands. At that time, I knew nothing about the Christian church or Christianity. I used to say I was Catholic. When I was a child, my grandmother occasionally took me to church. I made my first communion and did catechism, but that was it. My great-grandmother, Mauricia, was a spiritualist and midwife who made remedies for people. She used to travel long distances riding a horse when someone needed her to assist in childbirth. She also practiced witchcraft, but even so, she called herself a Catholic and prayed the rosary every day. If I were at her house, like when I went there on vacation or when my mother escaped my father's abusive behaviour, we needed to pray the rosary every day at 6 p.m. That was all I understood about religion.

When I walked into this Christian church in Carolina, Puerto Rico, La Iglesia Fuente de Agua Viva, I was struck by the fact that I saw no saints, statues, or candles, just an empty cross on the back wall of the altar... But in this Christian church, the people seemed cheerful, trusting, and friendly. I needed that. The preacher greeted us and preached with so much love and fire. I don't remember the content of the sermon that day, but I do remember the invitation to go to the altar if we needed help, to change our lives, and if we needed peace, in short, if we wanted to receive Christ into our lives. I knew I needed all of that, and I ran unashamedly, teary-eyed, straight ahead, where I was given a big hug and led in a prayer to invite Jesus Christ into my heart, forgive my sins, and give me eternal life. I cried like never before, but this time of joy, the joy you feel when you receive good news or when something good and great happens to you. I felt freed from the heavy burden that I was carrying. Something supernatural had happened to me. I felt loved for the first time. Something different had happened, arrived, or entered my life. I didn't understand much about being born again and receiving God's salvation and all that, but I knew something supernatural had happened to me.

What a glorious day to be sealed with this inner life, with this eternal covenant! The Bible says,

For God so loved the world that He gave His only begotten Son, that whoever believes in Him should not perish but have eternal life. God did not

send His Son into the world to condemn the world, but that the world might be saved through Him. John 3:16-17

Almighty God became flesh not to condemn us but for us to live eternally in Him. He paid for our sins and transgressions. He came to show us the way to the Father and how to live in the Kingdom. He is our sacrifice, the ransom for our sins. Thank you, Father.

I received the Lord in my heart, invited Him into my life, and asked Him to forgive my sins. The pastor guided me to pray. I had no idea what that meant, but I knew that something new and good had happened inside me. Immediately, a group of people came over to hug me, they took me to a room to talk with me for a while and get my information. They welcomed me into the body of Christ and gave me some pamphlets and materials they wanted me to read. It was an unforgettable day. I still struggled with the fear of being in a new and unfamiliar country, but the church inspired me; it was an oasis where I felt loved, accepted, and welcomed.

When I returned home, my partner was waiting for me. Oh, God, how depressing it was to come to that gloomy house after I had been in church in a beautiful and joyful environment and to have to look at that man and hear his threats under his breath. That day, when I arrived with his son and his wife, he was quiet. He didn't dare say anything because his son was present. That day, I told him that I had gone to church, prayed, and given my life to Jesus.

Usually, the fights and wrestling began at night. When I was in the house, he would get aggressive and yell at me about anything. I didn't go anywhere alone, except to the supermarket, which was very close to the house. In that house, everything was old, dusty, and dirty. He and his children were not very clean either. Life got worse when I complained that he hadn't been honest about his lover. His children informed me that this woman knew about me and hated me to death. Miraculously, I was protected from being killed by this woman. I later found out that she had threatened him and told him that he should leave me immediately.

All the men from whom I received violence and abuse were of the same line, so to speak. He was also rude and violent. He had a lot of rejection and bitterness in his heart. He said to me that he used to be a Christian and go to church with his first wife many years ago, but when I met him, he was far from it; there was not even a trace of believing in God; it was toxic.

Going back to the night I received Christ, I had a glorious time in church, but the flames of hell were lit in that house when I came back. I was worried for my life. I was new to a strange country with no family, and everything was unknown to me. My crazy decisions had brought me to the brink of death many times. Now I understood how stubborn and foolish I had been, and the leading cause was rebellion because of hidden pain.

When I was around this man, I felt like I was being oppressed. Everything was twisting in my guts. He looked like a real ogre to me, and I knew he was using me only for his satisfaction and pleasure; it was disgusting. I was living a double life, but inside, I didn't want to be like that. I went to church whenever I could and started taking classes for baptism.

I wanted to know more, and it felt good to know that God was my Father, that I had a Father who loves me and cares about me, despite myself, without expecting me to be perfect. But, at the same time, I wanted to get out of this man's life: "Maybe I should leave him and go back to my country," I thought. After all, I missed my culture and my people. At the same time, I felt that something new had happened within my being, but I didn't know what to do with the external or natural struggles in my life. It was as if I were broken in two. Sometimes I felt terrible fear because those entities and powers that I had sought and believed in before were furious.

After all, I had taken a new path; now, I belonged to Christ. But I didn't know much about deliverance or how to confront those entities. I had no revelation of who I was in Christ, nor about His love and eternal grace for me. I began to learn how to speak to God and asked Him, "Lord, deliver me from all that has persecuted me." I felt a beautiful presence when I was alone and talking to God while attending church. But the closer I wanted to get to God, the more tense the situation in the house became. This man's outbursts of anger were unbearable.

I now understand that when we have hurts and traumas and have been deep in darkness, when we receive the Lord, all hell breaks loose against us. Sometimes, it seems like we have not done anything good by receiving the Lord, but it is time to persevere in what we are learning and not let go of the Lord's hands.

We need to talk to God (pray) and learn His Word to help us stand firm and grow through it all. Sadly, many of us give up and abandon the faith before we grow up and are fully healed. We need discipleship.

Time to be baptized

Amid everything that was happening, I started school to be a hairdresser. I still wanted to improve my life, but I could not continue it due to a lack of transportation and economic support, and the school was very far away. Later, I learned to drive, but I didn't have much freedom, as he took me everywhere I needed to go in his car.

It was time for my water baptism three months after receiving Christ and a quick basic discipleship training. The day of the baptism arrived, I left the house with a great disagreement and argument beforehand with that man, but I managed to go to my baptism. I paid for a taxi to go to church, and from there, the pastor took all of us who were going to be baptized on a bus to the beach with great joy. As I waited my turn in a long line, we were asked to speak in languages if we were already baptized with the Holy Spirit, but I didn't know what that was, and I began to babble. The pastor and the co-pastor were in the sea waters baptizing everyone. I was excited, expectant with the faith of a child, waiting for my turn. Finally, it was my turn to enter the waters, and boom! They immersed me in the water, prayed, blessed me, and confirmed my confession and commitment to the Lord.

Oh, my God, I came out of the waters weeping and speaking in tongues, like a machine gun. I couldn't hold my tongue. It was no longer me babbling but an incredible inner force going outward. I still remember the experience as something supernatural. The Lord sealed my life. I knew I would need it, with all that awaited me in the days and times ahead. God seals those who are His. I remember the pastor saying, "You're blessed. God has great things for you."

I came out of the water so happy, bubbles of excitement jumping in my stomach. Then we got on the bus to return to Carolina, where I lived, in Castellana Garden.

I thought inwardly: Father, go to that ugly house with me. "My God, what should I do?" Could you help me? I was talking to God. It had a bittersweet taste; I was very emotional. I was sad that I had to return to that house where I felt that death surrounded me, and I had no peace; it was that serious when I used to get to that house. I saw my life at this point with two sides: the beautiful side that I had recently received, and the dark and heavy life from living with this man. That was my spiritual and earthly reality.

I must admit that all this was the result of my decisions, of my stubbornness and human folly. I hadn't been a little angel at all. I don't want to play the victim here. I made decisions on my terms, how foolish I was, my Lord!

When I got home, I decided to do our laundry. I was about to put the clothes in the washing machine, and the floor was wet. The old machine was outdoors and had four rusty metal legs. My mind was distracted as I slipped, and my left foot got stuck between one of the rusty metal legs of the machine, and my foot split deeply between the second and third toes of my left foot. A deep wound appeared between them. The strange thing is that part of my foot was split in two, but I didn't bleed a drop. I don't understand, maybe that part of the foot doesn't bleed when cut, or the fatty tissue prevents the bleeding, or it was God who didn't allow me to bleed. For me, the last explanation is true.

I was taken to the hospital and spent the rest of the day waiting to be treated. They cleaned my wound, gave me several stitches, and sent me home. To me, this has some meaning in the spiritual world; my steps were divided.

I want to say that things got better after my baptism, but that wasn't the case in terms of what was happening in the house and with my partner. It was an evil force stirring everything against me for the worst. It was hell at high tide for me. I was tempted to think that the decision I had made to accept Jesus was not the right one and had been in vain. I felt cornered just thinking that I had to deal with the person I was living with. But this time, I was deeply committed to being different and improving my life. I didn't have much knowledge; I was new to the faith, and I didn't understand many things about spiritual warfare and the spirit world, dealing with it from a wounded soul.

Something new inside me

There were emotional and physical mountains that I didn't know how to deal with.

Throughout my life, I had so many mountains in my path that something wanted to take away my strength for me to give up, but that little voice inside me patiently made me keep going. Everything was beautiful when I was inside the church, but when I left, everything was a whirlwind.

I wanted God to change me immediately. "What do I do with all this? May God come and solve these problems for me! Hurry, Lord! What decision should I make? I don't want to be separated from these beautiful feelings and this new faith that I feel inside me; what do I do, my God?" I used to think.

Many believers like me have faced tremendous storms after giving our lives to the Lord for different reasons. They face problems with themselves, with family, with spouses, with children, with society, and with many others, and they fail to persevere in overcoming them. Likely, the problems were there before we came to the Lord or were the consequences of our own decisions, but now they become more intense. The enemy raises *all that to make us retreat. It seems to be one thing after another, but all of that will pass away in victory if we persevere, believe, grow, let the Holy Spirit set us free, guide us, and let go of the past.*

The church must disciple new believers and teach them the Word of God and how to live by it. We need teachers and mentors who do not judge, but support and encourage us. They not only understand the Word and how to preach it, but also have first-hand experience, love, and patience to invest in new believers. Sometimes, we need people to pray for healing, restoration, and deliverance in our lives. We cannot live alone or achieve victory by ourselves. God does not want us to live like loner rangers.

Options for running away

After baptism, I found a job at a fast-food restaurant. I remember my whole being shuddering when I saw myself cleaning floors, cooking, washing dishes, trying to deliver meals, and serving customers. In those days, it was humiliating and embarrassing for me. I come from a culture where appearance and the status quo are important. Today I understand that all work is honourable and dignifying. Now we live in a society that judges less by the type of work you do. That job taught me humility.

While I was going to work, I was planning how I would leave this man and where I should go. Things were getting worse in our relationship in that house. I feared for my Life. This man became extremely violent and wicked. He punched me once during an argument, and I didn't want to be with him. I didn't have a friend I could trust and connect with on that island. I was a newcomer to Puerto Rico.

I called someone from the Dominican Republic and asked for help, but I didn't want to go back because I wanted a better future for myself. After having sold all my belongings and having told all my friends that I was going to Puerto Rico, coming back empty-handed would be a defeat and a shame for me. I was so silly and stubborn, but at the same time, fragile and vulnerable. I was in my early twenties at the time.

I called my uncle Andres de Jesus in New York and told him what was going on, that I feared for my life and that I wanted to find a way out of Puerto Rico. He travelled to the island and came to the house for a day, but I wasn't there when he arrived. He found Delfin with his rough and hard-looking face in the house. My uncle asked him where I was at the time, and he went and dropped my uncle off where I was working. My uncle said to me, "That man has a lot of violence inside; you have to get out of that house, or your life is in danger."

We talked for a few hours. He offered that I could go to New York, where he and Francis, his wife, lived. I thought about it, but it was very risky. This man would find out and possibly go looking for me. I got scared and started thinking about all the details. When I leave him, I don't want to see him anymore, I thought.

My uncle only came for a day and then went back to New York, thinking that I would decide to go to his house.

I appreciated my uncle's offer to help, but I wasn't sure.

I had to think about where to go so that Delfin couldn't find me. I contacted someone in my country, and this person gave me the name and address of someone who could facilitate my refuge in Miami until I could figure out how things would work for me. Miami, Florida, seemed like a better idea than New York.

Fear is demonic, and the enemy of the soul manages people through fear, using wounds and traumas from the past.

It's time to take off again

I quickly asked my contact in the Dominican Republic to buy me a one-way flight. One morning, I waited for my partner to leave the house, and I took a taxi, heading to the airport. I didn't tell anyone that I was going home. I arrived at the airport shaking and agitated. I thought someone was following me; maybe he had someone watching me. I had been paranoid since my youth; fear had taken over my life, and it wasn't very good. Everything was overshadowed by fear. Today, I know that chronic fear is instigated by evil.

Fear comes from hell itself. Faith comes from the Lord.

Something to ponder:

Faith comes from God. Fear attracts everything tragic and negative; faith attracts God, goodness, and light into our lives. We must be freed from the spirit of fear. We must willingly and faithfully break the bonds with that horrible spirit that is fear. It can be done.

I flew to Miami and left behind the church and those people who were from a slightly different culture but were Latinos like me, with the love of God in their hearts. Maybe they never knew the violence and horror that I experienced in that house. I was struggling with two extraordinary forces in my life, and I was unaware of what was happening. I know that inside was the seed of something good, but with my mind, my feelings, and my emotions, I felt a whirlwind of confusion. I had no one to confide in or ask for guidance or help.

It is essential to renew our minds with the Bible and ask God to reveal it to us in our spirit.

New believers need to have one or two people they can talk to and ask for prayer, be honest with, and learn from. It is essential to learn to pray and speak to the Lord continuously without fainting in those early days.

Jesus entered our spirit when we received Him; the payment for our sins has been made. He is the Way, the Truth, and the Life. His sacrifice is sufficient for the forgiveness and redemption of our lives. Spiritually, we are in Him; that is our position in the Kingdom, but our souls and minds need to be renewed and healed.

Our minds are renewed through gaining knowledge and asking God for His revelation. Even so, the process of transformation takes place throughout our entire lives on this earth. We go from glory to glory, and for that, we must believe and receive the benefits of the Cross. Every day, we should learn to have a relationship and communion with the Lord and renew our minds. It may seem challenging to some, but it is possible through the Holy Spirit.

You and I must be intentional in seeking the Lord and wanting to be transformed by keeping our focus on Him. Our enemies, Satan, the world, and our flesh or desires, are trying to push us back; the greatest enemy is our flesh, our soul, our mind, our self.

"Do not be conformed to this world, but be transformed by the renewing of your mind, that you may prove what is the good, acceptable, and perfect will of God." (Romans 12:2)

We need to renew our minds with God's Word. Our entire disk in our head needs to be replaced with a new set. When we decide to disobey and be stubborn, as I was, we do what we like or what suits us, we don't pay attention, we don't practice what we are taught, we make our own decisions, we become foolish, we get into dangerous spaces, and we have serious consequences for it. I also recognize the need for dedicated people who live honestly and wholeheartedly before the Lord to pray for us and with us for deliverance and inner healing. In Christ, there is not only salvation but deliverance, inner and physical healing, purpose, hope, peace, joy, and hope. He is our complete gift. But we must receive that gift by faith. I wanted to do good, but I had many ties and traumas. Even though there is life and hope for those of us who have truly given our lives to Jesus with sincere and repentant hearts, we still make decisions that are not under God's will; we make decisions in our carnal, old nature, in our old self. There is hope. The Lord promises never to leave us nor forsake us.

Wounds and damage in our souls infect others. Anger and violence pollute others if we don't heal. It's like we're spreading mud everywhere we go. He who is hurt, hurts others. We cannot give what we do not have. We give what we have inside, good or bad. The Father made provision through Christ for us to bear good fruit, but we must willingly surrender and die to self. I was one of those many people who are so damaged that they don't let God take care of their lives or their souls completely. I now know that, in the Kingdom of God, one experience is to come to Christ by being born again, and another is the transformation of our minds and our lives by giving everything to Him, taking up our cross and following Him daily. One day at a time. Some of us may take longer than others to surrender fully.

We need to come to the foot of the Cross to say, "Lord, I don't want to oppose You anymore. I give You everything: my mind, my heart, my body, what I have, and what I am. Your will be done."

Seriously, it took me a long time to realize how beneficial and blessed it is to surrender completely. My nature and wounded soul resisted everything about submission, obedience to God, and living in holiness. My soul resisted everything. My struggles have been mostly with not giving up and with not having faith, to let go and let God work. I needed to stop being foolish and stubborn and obey God. But it was far from that. I mean that every day that we are alive is a constant surrender to the Father. Day by day, we need to grow and collaborate with the Lord so that He will form His character in us. Yielding to Him is the key.

The Word says, "He who began a good work in you is faithful to accomplish it." (Philippians 1:7)

He will perfect and complete it. But He needs our cooperation and our desire and commitment to be what He wants us to be. God does not force anyone. I must admit that, in my early years of receiving Christ, I wanted to do things my way and tried to use the Lord as my Santa Claus. He loves us and wants the best for us. Yes, the Father has already made provision through Christ, but actions have consequences, whether good or bad. The Lord gives us free will to make decisions and challenges us to choose life.

"Heaven and earth I call today as witnesses against you that I have set before you life and death, blessing and curse, choose therefore life that you and your descendants may live." (Deuteronomy 30:19)

"Everything a man or woman sows they will reap." (Galatians 6:9)

I have experienced many negative consequences in my life due to decisions made from my soul, often with many unhealed wounds. As you keep reading, you'll understand why I talk about the great stubbornness and foolishness in my life.

CHAPTER 5

I ENDED UP IN JAIL

In early 1987, I arrived in Miami the United States. It was a new freedom for me. I had already felt this freedom, but what awaited me in this country?

There were many Latinos or people who spoke Spanish in the area where I lived at the time. The person who picked me up at the airport was kind enough to help me and take me to his house. Many people of colour lived in that area; above all, English predominated. I liked this new place; there were lights and lots of fresh air currents, and I could breathe at least natural freedom. This person welcomed me and gave me some advice. The first thing I did was enroll in a school that was across the street. I wanted to learn more English and become a bilingual secretary. I have always liked to study and learn; I have been a good student since my childhood, and I like books. I went back to school; I put in a lot of hard work and dedication to master the new language.

I used dictionaries, newspapers, cartoons, movies, English music, etc. In my home country, I had taken English classes, and I even once worked as a bilingual receptionist. Still, it was another thing to be in a country where the primary language is English, and each state has very different idioms and accents from each other. It wasn't very easy for me, but I like challenges. I've always been good at learning; I just regretted not having the resources and help I needed, but it's never too late to start over. I missed the church in Puerto Rico and how good I felt when I was in that church. I started looking for a new congregation in Miami and found one where I was welcomed with God's love, but the difference showed, at least in my heart.

Changing a congregation or community too fast can affect a new believer. Building down deep roots in a place, being disciplined, and guided is crucial in the life of a new believer. We cannot live as lone rangers; we need each other.

At first, most of us have a powerful spirit of independence, but we need to grow and strengthen with the intervention of the Holy Spirit and with the support and help of others. God made us to live and grow together as a church. There is a time when we must change places and move on if it is God's will that we do so, but we must make sure that it is under His direction and in God's timing.

Moving too soon from your community or church can cause the new believer to disconnect and lose track of their new faith if we are not careful.

I began attending my new church on Sundays, but my heart was no longer as fervent as it had been in the first months of my conversion. When I arrived in a city as big as Miami, the lights, the nightlife, the colours, the music, the parties, the fancy things and the extravagant way of life around me, it was another environment. My soul was still not surrendered, in addition to the anxiety that comes with the need for a job and to get ahead financially. I slowly began to lose interest in going to church. I had to call to be picked up to go to services. I didn't have transportation, and it was quite an odyssey to go to the Hispanic church. I stopped calling for a pickup altogether.

I enrolled in school to train myself so I could get a job. I hadn't finished high school at the time, so I needed a technical field. After a few weeks, the person where I was living already started showing signs that I had to move. So, I started looking for work, and then I found my first job as a cashier and assistant at a gas and grocery station. I was happy to have a job. So, I started helping my mother by sending her money frequently. I was paid relatively well at work. I was still studying, but my newfound faith in God was beginning to weaken. Work, school, homework, and studies, with only a few months in Miami, were a lot for me. I started looking for a room near work to move into. I no longer had the desire to sit or kneel to pray; I was losing interest in cultivating the new life and seed that was within me. In my mind, sometimes I had worries and fears that the Puerto Rican man would find me. I knew that he went to look for me in the Dominican Republic; he was locating all the people he knew, trying to find me, including my uncle, who visited me in Puerto Rico. One time, he even came to pick me up at my mother's house. I was better and safer in this place where I was now, with no one near me.

I found a person renting a room, a very charismatic man. He invited me to come to his house. He was a very kind man, smiling and friendly. He showed me his beautiful home, with big and expensive decorations and many images of Catholicism and other beliefs, Buddhism, Santeria, and others. Inside me, a red flag was raised that I didn't like very much, but I needed to move. I didn't know anyone else in that country, and it was urgent. So I rented the room. The job was close to me, and to go to school, I took a taxi. It was not that far, or I asked the owner of the house to take me to school, and I paid him. I finally had my place, and I paid for it monthly, which made me feel freer. After I moved in, I found out that the owner of the house was involved with someone of the same sex, which was his lifestyle and sexual preference. Artists and people knew him in the entertainment world as a friend. He liked lights, private parties, young men, and everything else. I don't remember seeing him doing drugs or drinking too much. But here I was, not knowing this man; I moved into his house, and I don't think I had many options in that new country either.

He was wounded for our transgressions, He was crushed for our sins; the chastisement of our peace was upon Him, and by His stripes, we are healed. (Isaiah 53:5)

Indeed, Jesus paid for our transgressions and sins, but there is a process of renewing our minds, surrendering our souls, and healing that must occur in our lives through believing and receiving His Word. Some of us grow and mature quickly; others, like me, it takes a long time, and many processes must happen within us. Because each of us has a will to make decisions, we have a soul that needs yielding, and the mind must be renewed with God's Word.

Lack of knowledge will cause you to perish; that's what the Bible says:

"My people perish for lack of knowledge." (Hosea 4:6)

Additionally, if we already know something, neglecting to obey it will also affect us. When I received Christ, I was marked for eternal life, and my spirit was positionally united with the Spirit of the Lord. The truth is that I needed to consecrate myself and grow in the knowledge and revelation that the Word of God provides, just as I needed healing and freedom in my mind and soul, naturally as well. We are spirit, soul, and body. I had to receive all this by faith and walk through it, making better decisions and sincerely seeking the Lord. At that time, I didn't know all this—or rather, I would say, I had no revelation of it.

The owner of the house and I became, I would say, "friends," but he started to see me as the next person to showcase on his catwalks and to present among his friends of both sexes. He began giving me advice on how to dress better and how to make an impression in his social circle. He introduced me to people from his entertainment world. Among them was his sister Mercedes (I changed the name), who ran a bar in Little Havana, in South Miami. I think they had a plan. I never slept with anyone of my gender, and I never accepted his offers to meet and mingle with his friends, who were all bisexual or of same-sex preference. But we did go to meet his sister at her bar.

When I got there, I didn't like that dark place or the smell; it was full of men drinking, dancing mariachi and talking very loudly. This bar had an island in the center where its owner sat in front of the checkout, and many beautiful girls were standing and talking to

the men who sat around to drink. There were cubicles with curtains inside the place, also. Those who wanted more privacy could go to the cubicles. The men sat down to drink and invited some of the young women who were inside the canteen to drink and go to the cubicles. The women who went with the men to the cubicles received good money as a tip. The bar used to have a section called the dance floor. When I went to that place and walked in, I thought, "This is not for me" with those kinds of people. I didn't want to hang out with them; I was very determined not to have anything to do with that ugly bar. I met his sister, and we left. For days, the owner of the house kept talking to me and insisting, "Oh, Joselyn, you can have whatever money you want without having to sleep with any man," and so on. He would also bring other young women to tell me how much they made in a night at the bar and how wonderful their lives were. Every day I heard the same thing and how much I could earn in one night, until one day I went and, of course, I got myself a new job.

At my age now, I realize that after we decide to give our lives to Jesus, the devil works extra to distract us in our minds and souls, using whatever it is so that we don't live a surrendered or healthy Christian life, because then we make decisions based on our desire, needs, or emotions that bring disastrous consequences to our lives. We lose focus.

If we don't continue to draw closer to the Lord, if we abandon our new faith, if we don't pay attention, we will listen more to the voices of those who are used by the enemy, to our flesh, and ambitions, instead of doing God's will and listening to the people who teach us, especially *to listen to the Holy Spirit.*

I didn't want to have anything to do with drugs; I used to say that at the beginning when I moved to the United States. "I didn't come to this country to use drugs or get involved with drugs." Even working in a bar, I never used drugs; I just drank cider and wine. I knew it was the best thing inside me. A few months later, I got tired of working in that bar and started looking for another job. I felt disgusted; that bar was not for me. I wanted something better. I didn't come to this country to work in bars, I used to say. It was never my intention; it's the truth, but I ended up there. So, I applied for a job at the Ritz Hotel Plaza in Miami Beach, based on advice from someone. I got the job and started working at the front desk as a telephone operator. I decided to leave the bar. But before I left the bar, the owner introduced me to a lady who had a drug retail distribution, and through this lady, I met some men who used drugs and drank like crazy. I became intimately involved with one of them.

I remember my first time using drugs. These new people invited me to use cocaine, and I replied, "No, I don't use cocaine." They laughed at me a lot; they thought I was joking or pretending to be an innocent dove with them, but I had not used hard drugs up to that point. At least, that was true in my life. I had never tried or used cocaine, but as you can imagine, I got another bad score on my record of fullness. I gave up and tried, and I got trapped. Like I said, I got myself a new man. I was 25 years old, and I had done a lot of crazy things up to that point that I'm not proud of. Still, the use of cocaine was not yet on my radar, but here I was in the United States, surrounded by new people in my life and using hard drugs; living la vida loca (the crazy life), but my whole being told me that it was very wrong.

So, I turned off that little voice as I went deeper into that world, and I became addicted. I started to like getting together to use drugs with other addicts, going to parties and going out with my new prince charming; he was handsome, with green, bluish eyes and the face of a movie actor. In my work at the Miami Beach Hotel, I met many people with different backgrounds and lifestyles. I started attending the hotel disco almost every night after work. There I had everything: work, relationships, the disco, the restaurant, even the hotel rooms in case I wanted or decided to stay one night.

I quickly got deeper into drug use. So, I started missing work because I was too tired to work after staying up all night. My life was going like a whirlpool. Inside me, I had great emptiness and insecurities; I needed acceptance more than ever. Also, I had a very unusual sadness within me that was continually in my heart. Nothing gave me absolute satisfaction. I felt bad seeing myself in the hole, but at this point, I didn't know how to get out, and I lacked the willpower. At times, there was a terrible hopelessness in my soul, which I tried to extinguish with drugs.

The prince charming that I was dating suggested that I move in with him. A few days later, we were already planning for this. I used drugs secretly in the house, and I got more into the mud. I went from occasional use to using it constantly. My lover explained that to move in with him, I had to help him so that we could have enough money to rent the apartment we were moving into. I asked him how I could assist him. He explained his business, and I would help him by finding customers and delivering the goods to the places. I didn't like the idea very much; I was scared to death of the idea of selling drugs; it was enough for me to be hooked on consuming and doing a lot of crazy things every day. Now, instead of saving money like I used to when I started my job in the United States, I was spending everything I earned to support my addictions, but I was getting to the end of my rope. Once again, inside me, something was not right. I felt that little voice inside me, which we call a red flag. But hey, my head wasn't prepared to last long, and I didn't have the willpower to set limits.

It is crucial to set boundaries in every situation and relationship.

But to be realistic, people like me at the time, with so much trauma, pain, and addiction problems, most of the time, we don't set boundaries. Already in a matter of weeks, I was very involved in drug use and running around like a headless chicken. It didn't take me long to accept the offer to help him despite my reservations. We found a client, a young woman I knew, who supposedly needed two kilos of drugs for someone else. I told my boyfriend. He advised me to take one kilo first and then the other. However, before the day of the negotiation, he asked me to accompany him to his sorcerer, who would prepare some rituals and work so that we would do well in this project. He knew and consulted that sorcerer for everything in his life. According to him, that sorcerer was very good at his job. Everything inside me said, "NO !" I had already experienced very negative results from consulting sorcerers, fortune tellers, and witches. In one way or another, I knew inside me that this was not the right thing to do. By this time, I knew inside that all this was bad and that there was only one true God. What a profoundly sad thing it is when humans choose to silence the voice of the Spirit within us, the voice that speaks internally. My new partner repeatedly insisted that, for us to do well, we should attend this consultation with his favourite sorcerer, who was known for helping people succeed in business and attain prosperity and good luck. As I mentioned, I had a feeling that told me not to go there. Moreover, I had past experiences with witchcraft, sorcerers, and fortune tellers, and none of them had benefited me. It's just a matter of spending money and time on things that draw you deeper into darkness and open evil doors.

The spirits of death and destruction influence your life in various ways. While we believe that consulting them is a way to do good for ourselves or others, most people make the serious mistake of doing so out of ignorance. These actions can add curses to your life and cause you to become bound. When I was raped, my grandmother, in her good intentions to help me, after taking the rapist to court, also took me to a witch's house to seek help. I had already seen my mother performing rituals with lamps and candles, trying to charm my father to be good or to bring good luck. Culturally, in my home country, many people practice divination and witchcraft, and it is normal for them. After the experience of receiving Jesus Christ, an alert arose in my heart, but I did not have a definition of my new identity; with my natural soul in a mess, I struggled to say no. All those traumas, pains, rebellions, and even pride in my life had to be surrendered and healed, but that wasn't the case for me at the time. I had a strong will and stubborn character, and I didn't want to let myself be tamed by either. I didn't know how. It's hard to understand if you haven't been there.

Let's go back to my new partner's invitation to go to a sorcerer. At first, I didn't agree, but in the end, I reluctantly went with him. When I say reluctantly, believe me, I was very irritated and upset; I didn't want to go there. We went to the sorcerer, and he introduced him to me, but a part of me was not one hundred percent present in that place. The time came when we had to commit the sorcerer to do some rituals and put on some necklaces that we would wear for several days. I don't remember how many, but I chose not to wear anything; to tell the truth, all that was already repulsive to me. Something inside me said that wasn't right. Well, the day after consulting the sorcerer would be the day when I would be the mule to take the first kilo of drugs to a house, and I would commit to take the second another day, according to what my gallant told me. My partner wanted to make sure they would pay for the first one. I didn't want to do all the rituals that the sorcerer had told us, but my companion liked it with all his might. He was sure that was what we needed. Anyway, I didn't wear the necklaces or do anything the sorcerer said I had to do, but my partner did everything exactly as he was told. I felt so bad that night to see this man near me, with all those necklaces on, smelling like a cemetery. We woke up in the morning and got ready to leave the house where he had spent the night. We had to go and pick up the goods from the place where he had them, while I waited in the jeep outside until I received instructions from my heartthrob.

The owner of the house where I lived also practiced witchcraft. Early in the morning, as we were leaving for our destination, he said to me, "I dreamed last night, Joselyn, that something black; I'm not sure what was chasing you." He said something else, but I remember that in the end, I didn't pay any attention to him; I was anxious about what was planned for that day. At that time, I was using a lot of drugs, as I mentioned, even hiding it from my partner because I was consuming too much. I was already out of control; my mind was unstable. Truly, God's Word says that we become seven times worse than we were after receiving the Lord's mercy through Jesus, and then we fall back into the mire of sins and rebellion. I fell into a deep hole. When I first arrived in Florida, things looked surprisingly good: the big new city for me, the luxury hotels, and the new friends. Now, almost two years later, I was already battling a drug addiction, and it was quite different. I was drinking, using cocaine, and partying all night, but inside I felt empty.

Indeed, when we are not close to God, there is a void in our souls that can only be filled by our relationship with the Father.

As I said, my partner and I went to pick up the kilo. I waited outside the house. When he returned to the jeep, we went to the house where I was to deliver it. We arrived at where I would deliver the goods; I carried the package as if it were a bag of candy, without any precautions. I had no experience in selling drugs; I used it, but I had no experience in selling drugs. I never sold drugs. When I arrived, the person in the house, my "contact," greeted me and told me to wait for someone else. That person was supposed to come with the money. And then she went to the second floor of the house. She said she needed to take care of someone upstairs. I sat at a table alone with no one else downstairs. I waited for what seemed to be a long time, which was a little strange to me.

Why do I have to wait so long, I wondered. I was left alone on the ground floor while everyone was on the second floor. At the same time, my partner, who had taken me, stayed in his jeep on the nearby street, waiting for me. There I was, sitting with the kilo in front of me, waiting for whoever had to come to receive it and give me the money so that I could leave. After a long wait, two people came in with the man I had been waiting for. These two people were undercover policemen; they stopped me right there at the table and began to read me my rights. Others also arrested the people who were in the house upstairs, posing as relatives, the young woman who was my contact, and some other people. At the time I was arrested, my partner was arrested outside on the street, a block from where I was. They took us to jail and put us in different cells, and then I learned that the person I knew who asked for the 2 kilos and the owner of the house were police informants. They had a long history of incarceration for drugs, robberies and other charges, and they had an agreement with the local police and the state attorney to get out of jail to look for people to tip them on. Therefore, they received special consideration in their cases and were released.

This case was in the year 1988 when the Colombian cartels were at their peak, and the people who worked for them were rampant and at their peak in Florida and throughout the United States. The drug business was very lucrative but also hazardous for the informants and could cost them their lives or that of their families, but they risked their lives anyway; like these informants I mentioned, they just wanted to get out of prison. This type of informant looks for others who are in the same situation as them to push them forward; they collaborate with the State or the judicial departments, and they are free again to commit the same crime or, even worse, repeat the same thing repeatedly.

That is what continues to happen even today. At the time, I had only 2 years in the US. Back then, in the country where I come from, there were no open cases of drugs or people who consumed them as freely as they do today, at least that I knew of. By having a drug case, I learned how serious the drug business was internationally and nationally, with all the cartels and criminals involved in those years. Shamefully, I found out too late when I was already incarcerated.

I am not proud of my actions; I have repented, and I know that God has forgiven me. In my twenties, I was immersed in my world and dazzled by a lifestyle I never experienced, with a new freedom and a cultural style on another level. I was not interested in knowing how the drug trade worked or anything like that. I just wanted to be accepted and fit in. The police took us to a detention centre. The next day, we had to go to the first hearing before the judge. During it all, waiting to see if I could get bail to get out, my prince charming found a way to communicate with me, encouraging me to be quiet. "Don't talk, I'll fix everything," he said to me. I, playing the saviour, the sacrificed, did what he asked of me. I did not say anything; I didn't accuse him. I didn't even say that he was my partner or that we were dating at the time of being in front of the authorities. After all, he was involved with others who were big in the business, but I did not know them or have access to them; it was all a mystery and a secret on his part. I thought it would be better for me to stay silent. Truly speaking, the truth could turn into a tragedy, I thought. I didn't have much to lose, and I didn't have family in Miami, but I was terrified of the fear of losing my life, maybe not by my partner, but by those behind him whom I didn't know, nor did I know how much they could do. All this heightened my anxiety further. Here I was in the women's detention centre, with no one I could rely on, not even a true friend, deprived of liberty, obeying everything I was told to do, getting up at 5 a.m. with a loud cry: "Wake up! Wake up!"

At dawn, we had only a few minutes to eat; those trays of food looked like dog vomit. We had an hour to go to the yard during the day. We slept compactly, with two to four people in a very small room. I was chained every time I left the institution to see the doctor outside, at the courthouse, or anywhere else. Once, I needed surgery, and they took me handcuffed to the hospital. After the surgery, I had two officers—one on each side of my bed—and when returning to the premises, they handcuffed me again. I was limited to making two 10-minute phone calls, one in the morning and one in the evening. I was alone, with no familiar faces, connected to different types of women in those cells. Many were normal, kind-hearted people who had done something wrong. Others were advantageous and manipulative, wanting to take advantage of others and use everyone, the system, or whoever they could. Most of them were institutionalized, and they went in and out of prison several times a year. The owner of the house where I lived came to visit me and went to tell me that he needed to rent the room he had rented to me. He also told me that I owed him money for the months I was incarcerated; he said that he had taken some clothes that I had in the house and some pieces of jewelry and had sold them because he needed payment. Another person came to see me; it was a pastor who knew someone I had known as a Christian for a long time and who once visited my home country. This pastor had never met me personally, but he came voluntarily to see me and talk to me when his friend told him about me.

Those days were stormy and complex, although good things also happened despite the hardship. In the three and a half months that I was not using drugs, in that place, I disconnected from drugs in one fell swoop; it was not like today, where they offer people who have problems with drugs so many things that in the end, they take you from one addiction to another. You fall into the same or worse thing in a while. I started going to Bible studies and meetings inside the prison. I had a desperate need in my soul.

A dream with Jesus

Once there, after a few days, I had a beautiful dream. I was on a mountain meeting and talking with Jesus while He was reciting Psalm 70.

It was a wonderful experience. It was refreshing for me to dream of Jesus. I saw Him dressed in white; I didn't see His face, but He was with me, on top of a mountain, and just perceiving His presence comforted me and gave me peace. How comforting it is to know that Christ knows us before the foundation of the world, that He loves us, and that even in our states of stubbornness, iniquities, and rebellions, He cares for us and helps us. Unfortunately, many of us don't take the time to get to know Him, and others never want to surrender completely.

The natural consequences of our transgressions are devastating because we are responsible for our choices. But our Eternal Father is still faithful to us. The pastor who was going to visit me agreed to help me get out on bail, and he and his wife decided to put their house as collateral to secure my release. I thank God for all the human instruments He has used to help me throughout my life. How great God's mercy is!

Our actions bring consequences, but God remains faithful and merciful.

In addition to the house as collateral, I needed money for the state to allow me to leave on bail. As I could, I contacted my partner to ask him to help me pay the money, and he sent the money. He was released from jail long before me; he got a costly lawyer, and his people also helped him, even from the first motions of the court. Sometime later, I found out that he supposedly said that we were only friends, that I had asked him to give me a ride, and that he did not know what I had in my bag. They released him for lack of evidence, according to them. Who knows what else he said about me? I did not understand anything. I did not say anything about him; I kept quiet. After he got out, he sent someone back to jail to remind me not to talk and that he would pay the bail, and he did. I don't know if he collaborated in some way with the State. I don't know what happened that he got out so soon without any charge, or maybe he was just another informant or something like that. The truth is that to this day it's unknown to me. Thank God all that's past is in the past for me.

Finally, out of jail

A day before I left jail, I met a very friendly woman. She was also there for drug charges. I understand that there was a pattern in my life. Every time I got out of something or a toxic or harmful relationship, I got into other relationships or something that kept me at the next level of evil. I spent three and a half months in the women's detention center in Miami-Dade County, Florida. After several court visits, the judge agreed to release me on bail.

The pastor and his wife, without even knowing me previously, put their only asset, their house, as collateral. Yes, as you read it, their house as collateral. Without having anything to do with this case or knowing me well, these people agreed to bless my life and be my guarantors, and not only that, but they also decided to let me live in their house for a while. Lord, thank you for so much mercy and love throughout my life. I am destined to be blessed despite the enemy or myself. Things like that do not happen often, my dear readers. Finally, bail was paid. I needed to appear at least once a month in court. The pastor took me to his house, and I visited his congregation a couple of times. It was a small community church, but due to an internal problem between him and his wife in their house, which I will not elaborate on, I had to start looking for a place to go. I remember making promises to the Lord on one of those church visits, but I didn't keep any of them.

After a few days away, I went to look for the woman I had met just the day before she was released from prison. Guess what? She was released from jail to sell drugs outside again; she was also out on bail. I went to visit her and ended up buying drugs from her, taking them to the pastor's house, and using them in the occult. It is terrible what addiction does to human beings. How embarrassed I am now! At that time, with a criminal record, no good friends, no family and no one who cared, where did I go? I couldn't leave the country, or to put it in a better way, I could leave, but I shouldn't do that to the pastor and his wife. They would lose their house, and forever, I would have that conscience, and I would also have someone looking for me, the INTERPOL or something like that. Just joking.

I went back to my old neighbourhood.

I called my ex-landlord, who had the room, and he agreed to let me move back into his house. To my surprise, the household and the attitude of its owner were different; he was no longer the same as before. Probably because I no longer represented the gain in one way or another that I once did to him. That's what some friendships and bonds with the wrong people do. When you are no longer serving their purpose, they are no longer the same to you. It was already evident that I could not live in his house. Everything was different. It wasn't a very cozy environment now. After a few days, I fought with him and left the house, not knowing where I was going. This man sometimes acted like he was my boss or my owner, very controlling, and I can't stand manipulation. That night, I found myself on the street, walking on the side of the road. A stranger passed me by, stopped his car on the street, and took me to his house, where he lived with his girlfriend. They were also struggling with addiction; they were drinking, and they offered me a drink, and I accepted the invitation. We drank all night outside in their yard. The next day, I kept looking for a place to live. I didn't know what to do or where to go, and I had no money or food. I decided to call Mercedes, the owner of the bar, and she welcomed me happily at her house. Mercedes slept all day and went to the bar at night to work. Being at her house, you can guess what came next, right? She told me she needed me at the bar to help her for a while, that things were not going well, and that she would appreciate my help. Again, I wasn't pleased, but at that moment, she was the only refuge and the only way out I had.

She even bought me food. I agreed to go to her house and her bar to help her, but it wasn't the same there either. Honestly, I despised that place more than ever, especially now that there was so much going on in my life, but as always, I didn't say no or set boundaries. I was fed up with that life. I wanted to run away and start fresh, but where and how? I was undocumented in the country because my probationary residency had expired, and now I was awaiting court with a criminal record. I didn't want to keep living like this; I didn't want to return to my home country defeated, and my family back home had no idea what was happening in my life. I didn't want to go to church anymore; I felt dirty. Guilty and ashamed, and seeing the pastor's life with his wife during those days, I was at his house, which was very disappointing for me. His wife was a lovely, very humble lady, but they fought and argued constantly. He treated her like a piece of garbage, and he began to flirt with me when I was at home. By then, I was in a sea of confusion and emptiness; I didn't know what would become of my life. That is why I didn't have many options besides dealing with an addiction. On the other hand, life must go on.

Chapter 6
A narcissist as a partner

One day, after I got out of jail, the woman who had introduced me to her friends—who were also her clients and with whom I started using drugs—told me about an honest, mature (according to her) business person seeking a girl like me. I was back on drugs again. Mercedes's friend advised me to meet this man at his store, a jewellery shop. She suggested I buy perfume and say hello to the owner. At first, I didn't pay much attention; I wasn't interested in the idea. I didn't need another abuser in disguise—I was going through so much. Every month, I had to go to court for my pending case. That alone was enough to drain my enthusiasm. But I was alone in the world, dealing with addiction, internal pain, scarcity, and a lot of tension because I didn't know what would happen in court.

One day, I decided to go and meet him. For the occasion, I dressed nicely in white pants and an elegant yellow short blouse, showing a bit of my slim waist back then. I arrived at the place, greeted the man, and began to look at the display cases of jewelry and perfumes. A few minutes later, the owner asked me how he could help me, but I saw that his eyes were pawing with internal, sensual emotions. I introduced myself and told him who had sent me. That man was so excited and was genuinely kind to me. He gave me an expensive perfume, then asked me out, and I accepted.

That night, he came to pick me up. We went out, and he took me home. I thought, well, he won't call me after tonight because I didn't accept his requests for sex. I wanted to be kind and thank him for the perfume, so I sent tulips to his business. The sending of the flowers left him speechless, and his desire to conquer me grew. A few days later, we went out again, and he promised me the moon and the sky. He told me he was divorced; later, I found out that he was only in the process of getting a divorce and that he had separated from his wife due to many problems between them before we met. He and his ex had a lot of baggage from the past; they had a toxic, turbulent relationship and many issues. I told him a little about my life, but not much. I told my new man that I had nowhere to go and that I was living in Mercedes' house, but I was a little uncomfortable and wanted to move. Immediately, he asked me to look for an apartment, and he talked to a friend who owned a furniture store to get everything I needed in one day.

Back then, he spent $7000 on furniture, which was a lot of money.

We rented a small apartment in a good place. I was amazed and happy to have my place, even if it was small. I was tired of walking around without a sense of belonging. I was pleased to have a place of my own, although I had to pay a big price later.

I had only been in the United States for a brief time, but it seemed to me that many years had passed, and I couldn't travel, or at least that's what I thought. Two years had passed. I no longer had legal papers. At first, I helped my mother whenever I could each month by sending her financial support, then I decreased giving as I became involved in drug use, and my sense of responsibility decreased. I always thought about her and my siblings. From time to time, I would send them something or call them, but not like I did when I first came to America. It was 1989, and the two years I had lived in that country seemed so long. My new partner and I were loaded with emotional suitcases of insecurities, rejections, rebellions, and iniquities. He was a proud, macho man. I soon discovered that he was also violent, drank a lot, was a womanizer, and had a dirty mouth, constantly cursing. He was Cuban; his father was Syrian, and his mother was from Pinar del Río, Cuba. He had three children with his wife, and she was a santera; she practiced the Cuban religion, "Santería." He told me that he and his wife did not live together. So, I had a new rival, who was a witch. The curse of witchcraft followed me, or I was attracted to it.

Our first long trip together to Disney World, about 4 hours from Miami, was not very successful. There, in the middle of our honeymoon (sarcasm added, we were not married), we fought and said bad words to each other, only a few weeks after meeting and establishing the relationship. That set the stage for long years of violence, disrespect, strife, and exasperation between us. A few hours later, we reconciled at Disney.

One day, his ex-partner, still his wife on "papers" at the time, went to his business. I was around but not inside his store, so we did not see each other. She showed up with all her children at the store and began to argue with him. She was looking for me to beat me for meddling in her marriage. I thought they were divorced, as he had told me. She had filed for divorce before he met me, but when we moved in together and she found out, she accused me and blamed me for all the old relationships he had had previously. Now, she had a face to put to all his ex-lovers' names; in other words, I paid for all the broken dishes of many women who, before me, were in her husband's life. Their marriage was brutal and dysfunctional, and they were two extremely broken and toxic people. That day, I was protected again from the significant harm that this woman could have caused me, since she was furious. My partner was a dehumanizer and a narcissist. He was not easy to deal with. I knew that they fought a lot and were constantly reconciling with each other. That was his lifestyle. The same was true for me later. We were also two very hurt people with a lot of traumas.

His wife was heavily into Santeria; as I said, she consulted others and worked witchcraft for people. He was not far behind. I saw him on several occasions locking himself in the bathroom with the tub full of leaves, flowers, candles, and large amounts of tobacco, doing a ritual with reddish and watery eyes while invoking his saints and the spirits of his dead relatives and talking to them. I knew his wife bought a doll at the supermarket next to his business. I said, "This doll is the representation of Joselyn, and I will kill her." (Santeria uses dolls and paintings as a representation of a person to do them harm). His three children were angry with us. I was new to his life, but I was the only one who formally lived in the house with him, and they knew it. There was a lot of pain involved. My partner and his ex had affected their children, hurting them and talking badly about each other in front of them. They used their children as a punching bag against each other in their marriage. The divorce came out shortly after we started living together. He had money to help his children with what they needed, as they expressed it to me, but it wasn't very easy. They lived like other poor kids on the block; he was very greedy and tight with his money. They came to the United States from Cuba via Mexico, fleeing the Cuban regime at the time. They left Cuba with little. He used to tell me that it was difficult for them. He once told me that, amid the struggles in Mexico, they were crossing a bridge, and he was disappointed, and his little son told him, "Don't worry, Dad, God never fails anyone." And it encouraged him. Then, they managed to come to the United States with their children.

A friend helped him open his jewelry store. He started small but managed to prosper and became a rich and very stingy man. I suppose it was because it was challenging for him to earn the money he had. When I met him, I saw something good in him because he was also a significantly damaged child in his childhood, but he never tried to help himself or wanted to change. He was the son of an Arab father from Syria and a Cuban mother, which is why, in Cuba, they call this mixture Moro among their people. Luis's father was a businessperson who made a lot of money selling goods by mule in the cities many years ago, throughout Pinar del Río and its surroundings. However, one day, he left his wife with many children, and Luis was one of them. As a child, he had to shine shoes and sell what he could on the streets to help his mother. His mother washed other people's clothes to support her children.

Shortly after I became involved with him, the fights between us started, fueled by jealousy on both our parts. I couldn't work; I didn't have the proper legal documents, and he wouldn't let me. He told me it wasn't necessary, which was true because he was wealthy. Sometimes, Luis and I would fight for days, and after those fights, I would usually call the woman I had met just a few days before leaving prison and buy drugs from her. I often called him when I was in that house to pick me up. He didn't know what I was doing there. I pretended to be okay when he picked me up, but most of the time, I was high. It seemed like he didn't notice, or maybe I was good at pretending. My partner still didn't know about the case or the legal matters, and I didn't know how to tell him. We fought about everything.

I did not want to tell him what I was going through, nor about my drug addiction, but one day, I took a chance, picked up the courage and told him about the big problem I had with a criminal case and that I needed help in court. He promised to help me.

Throughout the year, I had to attend court often for motions. The case kept getting postponed. The state knew that someone or more powerful individuals than me were behind it, but they didn't have enough evidence. I refused to disclose that my ex-partner was directly connected to the owners or major distributors of the drugs and that he worked for those people. My accomplice went free; they didn't present the informants in court for their safety, and only one person remained involved in the case, and that was me. Like I said, I was terrified to talk, as my ex had warned me not to speak. So, I told my story to my new partner. He said, "I'm going to help you." He sent me to his witch. I was so desperate and spiritually dry that, this time, I did not care. This time, I no longer had a conscience or red alert warning me. I had different ritual baths and a spiritual coronation; you can imagine what happened after that. I got worse. I kept going to the woman who got me the drugs for guidance and advice because I was already getting into a deeper hole with all the pressure of this case, the fights between Luis and me, and all my internal struggles. His jealousy worsened. He was 20 years older than I was. I was drinking a lot again and using hard drugs in secret. He wanted to look for a lawyer whom he knew, but again, I went to ask for guidance from my supposedly friend. She recommended a lawyer whom she knew was very good. According to her, this lawyer never lost a case. I was able to find another lawyer because, at the time, I had my partner's financial support. Still, in my foolishness and stupidity, I sought guidance from that woman and chose the lawyer she recommended to me.

My observations:

When people with addictions or codependency leave a place, especially one where there is a risk of returning to the same habits and harmful actions that could lead them back to old addictions, relationships, or routines, they must walk away, leave everything behind, and seek different options and locations. Otherwise, they risk going back into the mess and undesirable behaviours or anything they initially wanted to avoid. This could involve a partner, friends, a neighbourhood, a job, or a city.

The advice is to escape from the place where you were or from toxic relationships.

Trips to the courtroom

Trips to court for motions were frequent. The state wasn't ready for the main court case yet, and they kept delaying it for about a year, which made me very tense. The relationship with my partner was one of the most challenging. He was a narcissist and exceedingly difficult to understand.

He had many unresolved problems, just like me. He was a controller and manipulator; he loved to curse at me and say bad, ugly words, and he was also extremely violent. After the fights, we started the reconciliation process once again, but then we went back to the same thing. A relationship with a narcissist is the worst kind of relationship because we are trying to become what they want us to be, and they never please, and it is a revolving door of chaos and exasperation. Despite everything, I wanted to be with him.

Many times, I was tempted to go back to my country, but I was afraid. That was my excuse, and the reality was that I didn't want to leave him, as we were codependent on each other. He tried to help me, but his help always came at a price. He would take it out on me every time we fought. He always reminded me how much he had helped me. While we could not live together in peace, with so many struggles, we could not live separated, either. On top of that, he offered economic security. It was a very complex, toxic, and turbulent relationship, but at least we lived free of financial worry. One of the worst things that happened when we fought was that my past actions came up in our arguments. I had told him about my past, and he mentioned it and brought it to the surface to belittle and hurt me. He was someone I did not understand; when I thought he was upright, he was downward and vice versa. On some occasions, I would take my bags and leave the big, luxurious house that we used to have in Miami and go to where I first found a place. Then, he would look for me, convince me to forgive him, and the whole vicious circle was repeated. The same circle that my mother lived in, I was living. In all of this, I was to blame. This is typical behaviour of a narcissist. At the time, I had no idea what a narcissist was. Now I know.

His ex-wife hated me even though she was already divorced from him. His children were upset with their father; therefore, they were also upset with me. I represented an economic threat to their future. Their mother passed on that hatred and resentment to her children. In my opinion, she poisoned them bitterly against their father, and he was not a good father. He used to manage and control everything in the house and in my life, from the smallest decisions to the most minor details in my personal life. I had to depend on him. He wouldn't let me go to his business often or work with him as I wanted because he didn't want me to know where and how he managed his money. He wanted me to be under his control.

With all this, the court continued to postpone my case. The evidence they had against me was that two officers found me sitting at a table with a kilo of cocaine. It wasn't me they wanted to catch; they knew that I was used as a mule. There were no previous photos, no phone calls, nothing; they wanted the big fish (big people in the drug business). Honestly, I didn't know any big fish, only my old heartthrob and the lady who sold me detailed drugs. I did not know anyone else, nor did I know the names of the people who gave it to him; then he took me to deliver it. I was the delivery woman or a "mule," as they say to people who carry drugs to places. I had an affair with my boyfriend, but he kept the connections of his friends or drug bosses a secret. I did not have that information; I never met them. I did not know where they were or how many others were connected to my partner. On the other hand, I did not want to tell the story in court because it was dangerous for me, as he reminded me when we got caught. Therefore, I did not speak. I did not know much about the drug business and how it worked at the time. We are talking about more than 35 years ago, in 1988.

There I was, going to appear in court like a prominent trafficker. My partner's lawyer did everything he could to prove in court that my old lover did not know what I had in my bag, and he just gave me a ride. I later learned that my lover went free and was not summoned to appear in court again. Someone had to pay for that kilo and for the promise to bring another one home, which is called a conspiracy. My charges were possession and conspiracy, which are felonies. I went to court many times because they were not prepared. While I was still waiting for the big day of the trial, my Luis sometimes came home to find me passed out from drug use, vomiting, and sick.

I was sick of myself.

There came a time when I was fed up with myself and everything. I had hit rock bottom emotionally and mentally. My life hung in the balance. I made a firm decision not to buy drugs anymore. I was agonizing inside and afraid for my future. I started not to want to use any more drugs. I was tired of living in that kind of world, even weary of using drugs secretly. My partner was also an addict, but only for work. So he went to his jewellery store from 8 a.m. to 8 p.m., and I was alone all day in the apartment. His life was about money; he used to brag about how much he had. That made him feel superior, and it also made me feel inferior because I had no money, not even family nearby. He spent many hours working, and I was alone, using drugs in the apartment. I realized that I was hurting myself. This man, despite his nature, was with me and seemed to refuse to let me go. I began to yearn for change. I was sick of all that, fed up with the kind of life I was living.

Chapter 7
I went back to church

As I walked near my apartment in the northern part of Miami, Florida, I would pass by a large church called La Catedral del Pueblo. I wanted to do something meaningful with my life. "I don't want to go on like this," I used to think. I felt a strong need inside. I wanted to get my life organized. I had a court case pending, and I wanted to make a change. One day, I went to church and discovered that they offered professional Christian counselling for free. I tried to get an appointment with the counsellor at that church. Something inside me kept telling me: "You cannot go on as you are." When I arrived at the church, I met Alicia, a sweet lady from El Salvador, an intercessor who welcomed me with so much love and invited me to the prayer group that she led that same day. Alicia and another dear lady in that church became like my mothers.

I met Mrs. Yolanda Eden, the pastor of the church, and other cherished people who began to pray for me and show me love. This church was one of the largest congregations in North Miami. I started to attend twice a week for prayer and the Sunday service. I carried a heavy load, including worries about pending court appearances and the unhealthy, abusive, and narcissistic relationship I was living in. I was far from my family; I had no real friends to turn to. As always, I found myself in a cycle in the same situation. I had nowhere to go or family to rely on. The only person I could turn to was my partner, and often, he was my enemy too, so my best option was to go to church. Honestly, I was going more out of desperation than genuine love for God.

The Lord uses our circumstances to draw us near or back to Him.

Sometimes, the worst times are the best times to give up or to begin to seek God sincerely.

I would go to church to have people pray for me. I didn't know how I would go to church to have people pray for me. I didn't know how I was going to find a solution or a way out. At the Church La Catedral del Pueblo, I started to meet and connect with genuine and sincere people of God. Jesus redeemed us, and positionally in the Spirit, we are with Him in the heavenly places. Through the finished work of the Cross, we are saved, and we have redemption and eternal life.

Jesus redeemed us. Positionally, in the Spirit, we are with Him in the heavenly places. By the finished work of the Cross, we are saved, and we have redemption and eternal life.

As soon as we sincerely welcome the Lord into our hearts, we are born again. Our spirit becomes connected to God. However, we need to renew our minds and seek healing and deliverance for our souls. We must learn how to live the Christian life through the Holy Spirit in our daily lives. It is challenging at first, but with the Holy Spirit, it can be accomplished.

From what I experienced, I believe that if we do not have teachings about the Word, about prayer for deliverance and healing, and how to receive it, especially at the beginning of our walk with God, we will easily fall prey to the same trap of the enemy, we recoil and wrap ourselves in the mud from which we came, or even worse.

When we give our lives to Jesus, inwardly, we will not be able to be the same again, and we will not be able to enjoy our habitual sins. When you get wrapped up in the mud or vomit of your past life, so to speak, life becomes miserable. We belong to God, but we can't enjoy this life, and we can't be happy in church or anywhere else.

For some Christians, the Lord has set them free in one swift moment, and they immediately start to bear fruit. They submit, they begin to serve, and they grow quickly and expand, but many of us need time, discipleship, mentoring, deliverance, healing, support, and all the help we can get, along with a lot of patience to work through all the traumas in our souls. I speak from experience. It cost me profound consequences and pain to understand this, to have a revelation of it, and to let God work within me, I tell you.

In this new congregation, I began looking for someone to help me and guide me in the right direction. It was a small start, but something was better than continuing as I was; at this point, I was desperate.

I was going back and forth, appearing in court for about a year, until the prosecutor recommended that I plead guilty; they gave me five years, of which I would serve two and a half to three years for good behaviour. I refused to plead guilty because I said that the kilo was not mine. I did not want to admit my guilt and responsibility due to my ignorance and fear; I was living in denial. The kilo wasn't mine, but the reality was that someone had to pay for that drug, and I was guilty, as well as my partner, for having agreed to carry the drug.

The court's ruling

The court day came after so many postponements. My lawyer told me, "My advice to you is not to say anything. I'm going to speak for you. Everything is going to be fine; I'll show them that they only used you," he assured me. I was nervous, and my Luis was scared, sad and anxious. I didn't want to be taken away from his side. To begin with, he never liked that lawyer. He tried to look for another lawyer, but I didn't allow him. After all, he was the one who paid for the lawyer, but I did not listen to him and preferred to listen to the recommendation of the woman who sold drugs that I told you I was buying from.

We had gone to a church service together the night before. Sometimes, before, Luis had come to church with me after I begged and implored him to go with me to Sunday service, but as we were on our way there, he started complaining and fighting. We had big arguments, and when we arrived at the service, neither of us wanted to be there. Emotionally, we were a disaster. But this time, the night before the trial, he willingly went with me. We heard preaching from Exodus 3, when the Lord called Moses out of the midst of a burning bush and revealed Himself to Moses as the Great I Am:

"When the Lord saw that he was going to see, God called him out of the midst of the bush and said, Moses, Moses! And he answered, "Here I am." And he said, "Do not come near; Take off your shoes from your feet, for the place where you are is holy ground. And he said, "I am the God of your father, the God of Abraham, the God of Isaac, and the God of Jacob." Then Moses covered his face because he was afraid to look at God." (Exodus 3:4-6)

I didn't yet have the revelation of God's Word, but I felt that message somehow related to me. We went home filled with mixed feelings and emotions after the service. Both of us sensed that something was wrong, and I was very frightened. I cried and asked God to help me and us. That night, I cried like never before; I knelt by my bed and felt as if something inside me was about to burst. I was broken, but I still believed I would be free from that court. I don't know how I thought that because, initially, I was lying, declaring myself innocent. My heart was telling me otherwise, but I resisted with my head. I should have admitted my guilt and told the truth as I knew it, but I didn't. Secondly, I was the only one facing charges; no one else was involved in this case, and the informants were free for obvious reasons. They already had a case against me, which allowed them to be free. My ex-boyfriend had been free long before the final court session.

Who would pay for the drugs they found? Someone had to, and I was the only one on record within the legal system. That night, I did not sleep; my current partner took me to court the next day.

On the morning of February 6, 1990, I found myself standing before a jury, judge, prosecutor, and others in the room. I was trembling, as if I were shedding leaves on a windy day; my hands were sweaty, my heart pounding, my throat dry, and my mind wandering. A memory came to mind: I was once again standing before an accuser, when I was about fourteen years old. But this time, I was no longer that teenage girl. I was an adult trying to hide my sins and wrongdoings by not being sincere, and I panicked. When I was young, they involuntarily stripped me of my dignity, leaving me exposed without protection from my abuser. But now, I was in front of a prosecutor, my accuser, who wanted to give me the maximum penalty because I refused to testify and not accept the deal. I was trying to protect myself and cover up all my mess. Going to court represents time and money for the state, so they deal harshly with people who do not accept their responsibilities or do not collaborate with them in a crime, and make them spend money and time in court, and all that entails. A few weeks before, they made me an offer. They (state, prosecutor and authorities) were going to give me some consideration, but I had to talk against my Colombian boyfriend, about what I knew, and talk about the others if I knew them and what they did. They thought I knew a lot about the big guys, but I was just one more stubborn one who believed I could do things my way and get away with it. What can I tell you, my reader? I was in such need of acceptance that I did everything I could to fit in and have someone by my side. In the courtroom, I had one of the toughest judges in the district, and in front of me was a jury that didn't know who I was. I was facing them with the charges of drug trafficking and conspiracy. Who knows what was going through their minds? They might have thought I was one of the major drug traffickers or part of one of the mafias from that era. Back in the

1980s, Colombia's large cartels dominated the business and even influenced some political and elite figures in the United States, but me? I was just a small-time mule, one of the little ones that were caught. In those days, only the little people, the low-level ones, were serving sentences. The big ones were hard to catch, and everyone else kept their mouths shut. My lawyer advised me not to speak in court, which sounded good to me. I did not know if I could open my mouth anyway.

I was scared, and it might have made things worse. I did not even speak good English and did not understand it well, especially when I was under pressure. So, I agreed with the lawyer not to speak in court. I thought he would do a decent job defending me, but when it came time for him to speak, he brought me down with good words.

When the section began, he began to explain my condition as an immigrant in that country, and what I had gone through, how much I needed to survive in this country, coming from a poor country full of dreams and ambitions; he talked about how I needed to do anything to survive, in other words, what I was doing.

What I understood was: "She is guilty, but for all those precarious conditions she has gone through, I ask you to feel sorry for her." He didn't mention my partner who provided me with the drug, he didn't mention that I was an addict, he didn't mention that I was looking for help, and he didn't mention my ex-partner; he didn't even say that we both agreed to hand over the kilo or that the kilo wasn't mine either. Anyway, it sank me and left me alive. He influenced, subliminally, to make the court believe that I was the owner of the drug (I didn't understand this until later).

Once again, I wished that the earth would open and swallow me up at that moment. During the court's recess for the verdict, it took a long time to decide my fate, I mean, hours. My partner and I were in a corner outside the courtroom, in the hallway, debating again whether he could send me to the Dominican Republic or anywhere else. I said, "No." Thank God that I rejected that offer, and now I am grateful that I made that decision because imagine, dear reader, if I had left that court and gone to hide somewhere else, it would have been an international case, and they would practically believe with certainty that I was one of the prominent leaders in drug sales and distribution, because I ran away. Besides, my life, if I had fled the court, would have been in danger. I would have been a fugitive. I think I had help from above not to make that disastrous decision at that time. Of all the other wrong choices I had already made in life, I did not accept the proposal and asked him to wait for the verdict. We already knew in our hearts that things were against me. I am sure that I would be convicted and with the maximum penalty because I did not cooperate. Oh, Lord, I was living in denial of the truth!

We returned to the courtroom after a long wait. I was shaking, the whole jury was looking at me, and the lawyer was the calmest; only he knew what was in his heart and what he had talked about with the state and agreed with them about me. I don't understand much about the law, but from what I heard from the interpreter in this case, something was very wrong. At that moment, the judge entered the courtroom, the jury stood up, and so did we and the others in the room. The magistrate, after receiving the decision of the jurors, pronounced my sentence: "Joselyn Altagracia Joaquín de Jesús has been unanimously found guilty of the charges of drug trafficking and conspiracy. Due to the charges, she is sentenced to a minimum of 15 years in each case to be served concurrently with a mandatory minimum." Oh no, again, my world collapsed! I started to sob and turned to where Luis was sitting behind me. He was moved and tearful. We looked at each other, and I lowered my head. Now, the court agents handcuffed me to get out of the place. The judge said that I had the right to appeal, gave me time to do so, and gave me the instructions. At that time, it was a minimum of 15 years of mandatory imprisonment in state prison and with good behaviour, I could serve about 8 or 9 years. The officers took me to a dark, filthy cell with two boards as a bench against the wall and a toilet, all dirty and grimy. On the other side, in another cell, you could hear the screams and foul words of other newly imprisoned men and women who shouted about all kinds of things: "I'm hungry!", "I need toilet paper!" "I need to make a call!" and cursed horribly. I waited for them to take me to the holding cell until they took me to jail. Now I thought about what had happened; I had a sea of confusion, anguish, fear and pain of leaving my supposed freedom, and even a way of leaving my life with my boyfriend, who sometimes felt like a prison, but who in the end, was all I had as I have been practically alone in this country.

The sentence was given in February 1990. The officers came and escorted me from the jail cell in front of the building to a smaller, quieter office to talk to the lawyer. My partner was waiting to speak with him, too. We were both devastated and sad. We did not know what to do or what was next. We just knew it was a separation from our relationship, and we didn't like it. The lawyer spoke of an appeal; therefore, there will be additional costs and many more expenses. I do not know what we were thinking because we got involved again in a commitment to appeal, to continue fighting with the same lawyer. Oh my God, sometimes we think we are smart, but we're absolute idiots.

"There is a path that seems right to man, but its end is the road to death." (Proverbs 14:12)

After that, I was sent back to the jail cell. I decided that I would not go to prison until the appeal was underway. Here I was, in the women's detention center in Miami, where I was staying in a gloomy cell, with people unknown to me, screaming, arguing, getting up in the morning with deep shouting from the officers: Again, I had a choice: I could go to prison and wait for the results of the appeal there, but I decided to wait in the women's prison, I was terrified. I wanted to stay close to my partner so I could see him every week. He used to come to see me and always hoped that we would live together again. We didn't give up, but we did things our way and fought with our strength.

Dreams and more dreams

While I waited for the outcome of the appeal, I resumed attending Bible studies and even formed a group to pray, read the Word, and help others. While I was there, God began to show me the heavenly Truth. I had many dreams and understood them, and I used to see many visions. I remember dreaming many times about being in the waters and struggling in them, muddying them with my struggles, trying to swim, fighting, and working in the waters. At other times, I saw the clear waters that seemed deep, and I was afraid to enter them. I looked for trees and climbed one of them as if I didn't want to join the water. I understood what it was, but I did not do anything about it.

It was as if my soul was numb and refused to do God's will. At that time, I did not understand deliverance and iniquities, and I didn't understand the renewing of the mind, but God began to show me things that I understood, and my eyes and mind began to open to His Word. I fasted and prayed, asking people to pray for me, including those from the church that I attended before my incarceration. I started to establish some roots in my walk with God, I read my Bible constantly, and I understood more through the brokenness that I was going through. I cried a lot, but I also felt joy inside, like clear waters that were cleansing me. I was happy to be able to help others in that situation with the Word and God's love flowing through me. I also began to understand God's love for me. The inmates and I shared our lives and supported each other. On one occasion, I fasted for seven consecutive days, and I drank only water. The guards and staff used to bring us food on a tray, and I would receive it and then give it to another inmate to avoid being seen as not eating, which could be interpreted as a rebellion or a protest within the institution. It was a great blessing to fast in that place. I had the same longing to fast before going to court when I was outside, and I ignored it. The result would probably have been better if I had humbled myself, acknowledged my transgressions and wrongdoing, and sought the Father with my whole being, ceasing to live a superficial Christianity.

Acknowledging our faults, sins, wrongdoings, hurts, and needs is the first step to proper recovery. To say out from my heart something like: I need help, I am wrong. Help me, Lord. Sincerely and humbly.

I asked for prayer from my beloved Alicia, who visited me often in jail. If you remember, I was searching for some peace and support and became involved with the prayer groups. She loved me and helped me a lot outside prison. I told her about the idea of getting married inside the jail because my boyfriend and I wanted to get married. Imagine how crazy, and she told me: "You're already here in prison, Joselyn. Why don't you wait to get married when you leave here and wait to see if it is the Lord's perfect will?" But I understood and believed that I should get married. What was I afraid of? I was so scared of being alone in this world, especially in jail, that I needed the support of someone like my partner there. And I paid little attention to her.

During my fast, on one occasion, I heard the voice of the Lord from within my being. I sensed this word very strongly in my mind and my heart.

In 1 Samuel 16:7-8, it says, "Do not see his stature or the beauty of his appearance, for I reject him." People look at the outward appearance, but the Lord looks at the heart."

But I was numb and oppressed, I would say, and I also silenced that voice. Flesh and minds are deceitful. We had the brilliant idea of getting married while we waited for the appeal of the sentence. A few months after I was sentenced, we were married in the jail's chapel.

The person in charge of the jail was a notary public, and here we were, the bride and groom, very excited to get married. Some inmates who became friends inside the jail sewed my dress by hand. My partner brought the materials for my dress and the head ornaments, and they made me a beautiful dress. He got a bouquet, sandwiches, and a cake to the women's jail with permission from the administration. Some privileged fellow inmates were able to participate in the ceremony. We got married at Dade County Women's Jail, right in the city of Miami. That day was bittersweet for me due to so many unknowns. We didn't know what the future would hold.

Being in jail feels like your whole life is frozen. The world outside seemed unreachable and unreal; it seemed as if my entire life had stopped and had no way out. Our days become the same routine. We reluctantly obey the authorities for fear of losing privileges, but inside, most of us struggle with anger, rebellion, and sadness. A short time after the wedding, the news came that we had lost the appeal, and now it was final. I had to go to prison, to the "big house," to serve my sentence. I was terrified by everything I heard from those who were serving time in prison and what was going on there. For me, it was another giant in my life I had to face. Everything trembled inside me, with more questions, loneliness, and insecurity on the surface, but I had to go to serve my sentence, and that sentence could not be served in the detention prison. We can only go so far. Prisons are usually outside the city.

Chapter 8
Prison time

The day arrived to go to prison, and I already had everything packed. They took me in a van that had internal iron bars inside for safety, along with some inmates. We arrived at a place where only iron doors and double bars of metal and wire were visible. It was a large building with guards outside, and in the distance, as we approached the place, I could see many women walking to and from, all dressed alike in the camp. After I arrived, I had to spend several days in quarantine. As a newcomer, I needed to spend a few days or weeks in a secluded place, separated from the regular camp population, to learn the rules and behaviour expected within the camp. Before entering that place, they gave me a full bath with special shampoo to ensure that I wouldn't bring bugs into prison. Here, I would no longer wear my regular clothes. I would have a uniform of two or three dresses, one or two blouses, a coat, two pairs of jeans, some underwear, a few pairs of socks and a pair of sneakers. We all had to work and go to school. At the end of my quarantine, I was assigned to work in the chapel. I went to work with other inmates who had worked there for a long time. I was told that the chaplain's wife also occasionally helped in the chapel. Later, I met her. She was a very kind woman. I joined the choir, and the chaplain's wife was the choir's director. She mentored me in my new role, as I wasn't quite sure what to expect. One thing I understood: it was a privilege for each of us to work in the chapel; only a select few could do so.

Well, a few days later, I started to like my workplace. It was so clean, quiet, and with so much Christian material, such as television, movies, videos, books, CDs, and much more. It was better than any other workplace within the institution. It was what I needed. The chapel staff had a small office near the chaplain's office. We had a TV, a coffee maker, and a small microwave. That was a great privilege back then. There was a library, where books were lent to prisoners, a lovely chapel for services, and a large room for activities. I was entrusted to clean and maintain the place. I cleaned the floors, polished them, swept them and cleaned the bathrooms very well. When I could, I prayed and talked with other inmates about Jesus. We held meetings in the courtyard on Saturdays, where I preached Christ, encouraged others, taught, and worshiped the Lord aloud amid the camp. I saw the Lord's hand and His comfort in the hearts of the inmates. Many came to receive Jesus as their Lord and Savior. Some of them are serving God in different countries, and I am still exchanging communications with many of them, glory to God.

I had access to all the Christian materials inside the chapel. I made a routine of praying and making time for God's Word after completing my responsibilities. My chaplain gave me an English Bible, the New International Version, and I said to myself, "Who's going to read this English Bible, chaplain?" It was too much for me because, at that time, my English was very limited, but little by little, I learned to read it. It helped that I understood the stories because I knew them in Spanish, and I started to read and memorize them in English, and even to preach the truth of God in English. Hallelujah!

Very important and real visions

In those times, I had more visions and dreams than I do now. One vision that is still vivid in my mind is a waterfall. I saw a bright waterfall of living water. My eyes could not look firmly at the waters because they were very bright, living and resplendent waters. I tried to stare at them, but I couldn't. I tried to read some words that hung over the waters horizontally in gold. I was finally able to look closely and read them. **I AM CONCERNED**

ABOUT YOU; I AM I. That vision and its meaning have been with me ever since, and it has marked my life forever. It also had significance to my circumstances. God introduced Himself to Moses as the "Great I AM" in Exodus 3. Do you remember the preaching of the day before I went to court? It was about "I AM."

I've had many significant dreams and understood their meanings. On three separate occasions, I heard God's powerful voice not from outside, but from within me, each time while kneeling in prayer and entering a state of ecstasy or numbness. Two of those occasions were instructions to me, and the third time, the Lord was correcting me, which didn't sound sweet, but as a dad, when He has to speak seriously, He does it firmly.

While incarcerated, I began contacting outside ministries and receiving free Bible study materials. I longed for more of God and had a passion for Him in my heart. My partner sent me everything they allowed me to have: earrings, a radio, perfume, some money, etc. I must admit that he fell in love with me in his way. He was also a victim of a lot of pain and trauma in his life.

I first learned to preach and teach in prison. I learned to give and tithe from prison as well. I used to take my share of what I received and send it out to a specific church or ministry, especially to poor children and people in need ministries.

I didn't have much at the time, but God only knows how much love and dedication I was pouring out in my offering to the Lord from within the prison bars. I learned to pray for my offerings and consecrate them, a practice I do to this day. My days and my life in prison were for God, to make my time the best I could, to call my partner and wait patiently to see him when I had my next visit. I saw him not every week, but every two weeks or so.

Shame for getting naked

Oh, my God! Having visits in that place was another challenge. I tell you, it was a great challenge for me. It was painful, embarrassing and agonizing! On the days that we had a visitor, they called us by name through speakers, and we had a few minutes to enter a small room where they searched and checked us. They made us strip completely naked and bend down and cough as many times as the officer considered necessary.

What a shame, especially when I had to bend down and open everything in front of a woman who looked at me as a man, who preferred women over men. She looked like a man, and to me, it was as if a man was strip-searching me. I wanted to die every time I had to do that. I felt very ashamed of having to undress as I walked in and out of the search room. It was a massive challenge for me internally. I have never undressed in front of a woman, not even in front of my mother, since I was a teenager. It was not a joke. That part of the visit was hard for me. But I was rewarded with the privilege of spending a few hours with the only person I had and who always came to see me, my partner. I was always jealous and consumed by the idea of my husband being out there with another woman. My insecurity was at its peak. I think it was an obsession, something demonic; the same thing happened to him. We were both in the same trap. We were constantly fighting over the phone because I was continually instigating him and blaming him for his actions or inactions. I imagined things and suffered internally; in other words, it was a toxic co-dependency. Not only was I trapped inside the physical bars, but also inside the emotional and mental bars. I was serving a double sentence. I needed a lot of healing.

Despite having received Jesus into my heart and even serving others in His Name, being incarcerated brought out even more of those insecurities and rejections within me. My partner came to visit me and answered my calls, but over time, he became indifferent. He began to change the way he dressed; he began to dress like a young teenager. He began to find the visits uncomfortable and missed the weekends when he had visitors.

Later, I discovered that there was a person in his life, a 25-year-old girl, about 30 years his junior. Knowing this brought me a lot of pain; I literally felt like I was between the sword and the wall, especially dealing with those emotional walls. Only when you experience it can you understand it. I decided not to give up my relationship with my husband; instead, I entered a spiritual warfare of crying out to God. I prayed and cried out. I fasted there inside the prison for that relationship so that my husband would leave that young woman. And even better, I wanted him to become a faithful Christian. At that time, he was worse with me than ever. Before, he showed that he wanted to be with me; now, I felt like he was disgusted when he came to see me. I felt so helpless, and it hurt. Many months later, he confessed that the relationship with the young woman had ended. "I never thought I would leave her at all," were his words. I had been in detention for four years. I always prayed to God to help me to get out of prison before the time I had to serve. I asked Him to have mercy on me and that I needed to leave. Looking back, it was not a good idea as I needed to wait on God and for Him to use His perfect timing for me.

Within the institution, I worked, went to school, served God, helped with chapel services, and participated in Christian activities and camps. I was an exemplary prisoner, thank God. I avoided learning bad behaviour from other inmates and refrained from engaging in common prison issues such as sex, drugs, promiscuity, manipulation, control, fighting, death, and violence. I saw women engaged in sexual relations with security guards, and harassment was widespread. Prisoners are sent to solitary confinement because of misconduct, suicide attempts, or attempts to harm others. Some change their sexual preferences drastically, regardless of their social status outside or their families' opinions or concerns. Others lie and try to manipulate their peers and the system as much as possible.

Thank God I stayed on the Lord's side. I sincerely wanted my life to change and to know Him. Despite my emotions and the burdens in my soul, I still wanted more of God. I kept learning. I learned to pray. I fasted, studied the Word, and helped others. I started to change and be different. By God's grace, I remained in His hands, not wanting to mix with things that I knew were wrong. I longed for the Lord in my life while having compassion for others. I used my free time to help others; every Saturday, we would gather outside in the center of camp and study the Word, worship, share, and pray. At first, I was praying alone, and then more people joined me every Saturday. Some of them received the Lord and received healing, deliverance, and encouragement there in prison. Praise the Lord!

Yes, you can be free in an institution or anywhere else if you want. I have always loved to preach the good news of the gospel. I had to do it very carefully because when the officers saw a meeting outside, they would start to panic. They were worried about an insurrection, but over time, they understood what it was, and they left us alone, especially knowing that I worked in the chapel. Praise be to God.

Some made fun of me or didn't like me because of my faith or what I represented to them. But everything was fine. I was an exemplary inmate, thank God, I never got into trouble within the institution. I was always respectful of the rules and regulations, as well as the officials.

I learned a lot and grew. When I had already served four and a half years, the Governor of Florida, Lawton Chiles, due to overcrowding in the prison system of the time, decided to commute the sentences with a conditional pardon of all those who qualified. The requirements were:

- That we had served a third of our sentence,
- There was no improper behaviour

- That we had no serious disciplinary measures,
- We had a deportation order from a judge

I had a deportation order because my conditional residency was already cancelled, and I did not apply for permanent residency when I had time out. Those who wanted to participate in the mass deportation and qualified had to apply, and so I did. I was selected, and the management asked me some questions, such as, "Joselyn, what will happen to your husband?" I was desperate to get out, especially thinking about him and his recently ended relationship, which still bothered me. I didn't want to separate myself from him anymore; at least he could visit my country, and maybe he would even move there to the Dominican Republic. At the end of the day, he had all the money and more than we needed to live well in my country, I thought.

The benefits of the commutation of the sentence were that I had to be deported to my country and not return to the United States for years. I consulted with my husband, and he agreed. I already had my decision, even though I was praying, and I had a red flag inside. I wanted that, and according to my mind and emotions, that was what God wanted for me. It was something to get me out of jail early.

I still had about three or four years left to serve my regular sentence. The prison administration did everything possible to get me out soon, and many others were also leaving with this new opportunity. We were going to leave the system, yes!

The day to get out has arrived!

The day came to leave for my country, and everything was arranged. My husband was happy, even though I was going to be deported and he was going to be free. He brought me suitcases with clothes, shoes, makeup, and other things. I was surprised to find my husband there when I arrived at the airport. He found out my flight departure information and bought himself a ticket to go with me. We were there on the plane, taking photos and videos. All went very well. When we arrived in my country, we didn't know anyone. It was a challenge for us to get to my country after my deportation. The immigration officers took me to the local officers, who took me to a small cell in a detention jail on the outskirts of the airport, claiming they needed to give me access to the system. Luis didn't leave me, not even for a moment; he was with me the whole time. We slept on the floor on a mattress in that small cell. We slept in a sordid and unpleasant room near the beach of Boca Chica for one night. Other prisoners were also deported. In 1994, if you didn't have anyone influential to pick you up and help you at the port of entry, the chances were you'd have a tough time and end up spending a lot of money. We would likely have to spend a few days in prison for the authorities to process the paperwork. But in reality, it was a way of getting money out of us that they would divide among themselves, between the police and all those in charge of processing me to go out to the public.

After they got me, they sent me to the police central department in Santo Domingo. When we arrived, they sent us from one office to another, from one cell to another inside the building, until my husband got angry and started shouting insults at all those police officers because he was upset about what they were doing to me. I had to ask him to calm down. The truth was, I had no criminal charges in my country, and none of this made sense. They let me out on the second night with the promise that we would return the next day. Fortunately, we found a high-ranking officer as a guarantor who helped us and took responsibility. The next day, we started the same routine as the previous day. The officers, in their pursuit of money, pretended to be helping us to get me out into the free world (that's what they promised in the first place), but it wasn't real help. In the end, we were told that this would cost us a specific sum of money to solve the problem. According to them, my case had to go through this department, the other department, and so on, and each department we visited wanted a large sum of money. At one point, my husband said that he would not pay anything else. He said I had no crime in my country, owed nothing there, and was coming back to my homeland, not to a foreign country. He was willing to argue with them like a Cuban who has an aggressive, viperine mouth. But he was right. I had a clear record in my country. Why all this, then? The answer? Money and more money. They used to make a profit from people in need. Many hours later, after great anguish and anxiety. They let me go free. As I write this, more than 30 years later, the system has changed a bit. After I got out, I called a lady whom someone had recommended to me while I was in prison. She was well known in her community, a woman of God. She received me in her friendly house and recommended another person who could accommodate us in her home for as long as we needed, because she had an empty room. I rented that room. These two women were sincere Christians, and together, we began a beautiful friendship in the Lord. God began to open the doors from day one, and I was free in my country. Two days later, after I was out in the free world, someone invited me to a radio station to give my testimony.

People who were related to these two women began to invite me to different ministries to give my testimony about my life in prison. I started preaching, volunteering, and helping at a drug rehab center. My husband returned to Miami, but before he left, he told me that he would bring me back there. My time with him in my home country was bitter because he didn't want to live there. He thought it wasn't up to his level, and he loved his business and his money in Florida. I wanted to be with him, but I'd be back in Miami and too soon. No, that was crazy.

During the few days we spent together, I felt we were very emotionally separated. We fought a lot and didn't understand each other. I wanted to serve God, and he was in his world, very different from mine. I didn't understand the man; he was a complex creature, and he probably didn't understand me either. We had been separated for four years, and much had happened between the two of us. For example, he had a relationship with a girl much younger than him, whom I already mentioned, and even younger than me. I was in the clouds, focused on my faith and how to serve the Lord and continue to grow in Him. My husband's ambition was to get richer, as he was distracted by worldly things. Imprisonment can destroy any good relationship, and our relationship was very toxic, complicated, and dysfunctional from day one.

The twenty-year difference between us was also unfavourable. Many other people and my family welcomed me to the Dominican Republic at that time. My husband was not happy to see me in my homeland and with my people. In his mind, I was getting out of his control. I went to visit my mom in the countryside where she lived.

I was happy, in part, to be free, but my heart was still attached to the relationship with my husband. I was codependent on him. He visited the Christian meetings with me to criticize everything and everyone. After flying to Miami, I was left with the promise that he would come back as often as he could. I tried to convince him to buy a house in the DR and live there, or to travel frequently to be with me, but he ignored me. I began volunteering in a drug rehab ministry where the Lord opened the doors for me within days of arriving in my country. The Lord brought many beautiful and kind-hearted people into my life who, without knowing me beforehand, believed in what God had done for me and in me up to that point. I will be eternally grateful to so many people of God, people who have influenced and helped me throughout my life. I also began to get closer to my son, Aneurys. He was in his adolescence, and I was able to talk to him honestly. I asked his forgiveness for not being with him when he needed me most. The Lord put in my heart words to express to him, and this began to heal his heart. We travelled together to my grandmother Flora's house and my mother's house in Moca, and we spent a lot of time together. We began to connect and heal.

Despite my family, my son, and all those good Christian people, in a little corner of my soul, I was sad for not being able to be with my husband in the United States. I didn't want to live permanently in my country; I wanted to be with my husband. I couldn't visualize myself without that relationship. I thought my whole world would collapse. My husband advised me to look for someone to help us return to the United States.

One day, we found someone who would help us and take me back to the United States easily. At first, it sounded crazy to me; that's not God's will, I thought. I was consumed by fear, knowing that this was disobedience. I was debating whether to go or not, and I entered into terrible anxiety. I was terrified to proceed with the plan. He told me, "Joselyn, your life is not the same. You're my wife, and you're not going to be doing anything wrong in Miami. You have to come back to me." He even quoted some verses from the Bible about the wife who should be subject to her husband. The man did not live for God, but he knew a few verses to remind me when he needed to accomplish what he wanted. At that time, you could do that and more in my country if you had the money and the right connections. At first, I was shaking and terrified, but I subtly convinced myself that maybe it wasn't so bad because I wasn't living for the world; my life with God was different now, and I was trying to be next to the man I was married to. I swallowed Satan's bait and deceived myself by lying again.

Now, as I write, my dear reader, I have this revelation: *Obedience is better than sacrifice. Half-obedience is disobedience, and the one who is most harmed is the person who believes a half-truth or half-obeys.*

Our wrong decisions and disobedience bring many terrible consequences. Complete obedience is worth much and saves us a lot of headaches. I realized this later, after much pain and many losses.

You don't have to go through the same thing, dear reader, if you learn from my mistakes, which is why I hope you'll find this book helpful. Our decisions cost us much in life. My husband left and returned a few months later. He agreed to pay the person who would help us. We already had everything planned.

Chapter 9
Back to the United States

My husband returned to Miami after we had planned and paid the man the money. Lots of money. I later flew to New York, and my husband was waiting for me at the airport. We started fighting as soon as I arrived. He stayed with me for a few days in New York. I visited my sister and wanted to share with her and learn more about New York, so I stayed a few more days, but then I went to Miami.

I flew to Miami a few days later. Here I was then, after several years, back in Florida. Things were very different. My husband was more distant and suspicious than before, and I was still very suspicious that he could go back to his previous partner. The reality was that he loved to get involved with young women and prostitutes. I was back, but I wasn't free. I panicked wherever I went, even in our own home. I didn't know if anyone would know that I was in the country illegally and call the police. We fought continuously, arguing and disrespecting each other. He was the first to remind me that I was illegal when we fought. He was the same man, angry and disgusted for no reason; he was bitter, with a lot of poison inside him. We were the perfect combination of emotional and spiritual luggage carriers. I went back to my vomit.

I interpreted his behaviour as if he were someone else. Clashes, fights, curses, and violence intensified. I revisited the church I used to go to before I was imprisoned, the People's Cathedral Church. I was happy to see them again, but I was scared, and inside me, I knew something wasn't right. I wasn't at peace. It's no joke to live under conviction. Our fights were tough, and he didn't seem to be happy that I was back in his life. He was distant, living a double standard, and I knew it. I didn't know how to handle it. So I started trying to force him to love me. I lost so much weight that I weighed close to 100 pounds, but nothing changed in our relationship. Instead, he kept humiliating me and making me feel like I was always at fault. Every day, he looked down on me, told me that I was not attractive, that I was already old, and always proudly talked all the money he had. Sometimes, I believed him and tried to do my best to please him and make him happy, but he wasn't pleased with anything.

This man was very complicated, and I tried everything to make our relationship work, but nothing worked. I thought that he would change if I prayed more and were more submissive. Perhaps he could find help, but he never wanted to seek help and go with me, because he thought the only one who needed help was me. I left my house several times and went wherever I could in Miami, to the houses of people I knew, or in New York to my sisters. Then he called me very softly and kindly, sent me money, begged me, made me many promises, and I returned to my house in Miami. On one of those trips to New York, I had the opportunity to help my sister, Iris, when she was expecting her first baby. I was in her house. I took her to the hospital when the water broke, and I was the first to see the baby coming. I also took care of my niece, Denise, my sister Magalys' daughter, when she was also a few months old. Taking care of my nephew at birth and my little niece at that time in New York gave birth within me to the desire to have a baby. I longed for another one. However, it had been about 15 years since I had my firstborn child. I didn't know if it was a good idea, but I wanted a baby. I returned to Miami when my partner became a sweet dove again. I got pregnant, and when I found out, I had many mixed feelings and emotions. I knelt to pray and placed my baby in God's hands. I had a complicated pregnancy; our relationship became worse because we started fighting physically and verbally. Sometimes, my partner would scream and even hit me, telling me that my baby was not his, to make me feel bad and irritated.

A voice told me to kill myself

By this time, my partner and I were already on the same level, as we both became very violent toward each other. Once, in the middle of an argument, I heard a voice: "Kill yourself because your life has no meaning, and you will always be the same."

I had stopped going to church to please my partner and see if things would change between us. There was no peace or quiet in the house anyway, and things got worse. When we fought, we would go to separate rooms. That large luxurious house with marble floors, a patio, a large pool and a jacuzzi was a place with a heavy and dark atmosphere.

On that specific day, a heck of a fight broke out between us, with all kinds of shouting and swearing. That day, I was able to discern whose voice it was, but instead of obeying that voice, I came to myself and cried out to the Lord in prayer and tears; and peace came to my heart and my home, at least momentarily. My partner's children were supposedly okay with our relationship, but it seems to me that they had a different agenda. (At the time of writing, we have good communication and interaction with each other.) Honestly, I wanted them to be closer to us, but my partner didn't want them to be close.

I did my best to open the doors of our house and welcome his children, but at that moment, they were not ready for it. Their parents so hurt them that they didn't know how to accept love or let go of resentment. Thank God that today is a different story between us, because I decided to forgive them and love them.

Jesse was born

I was happy to be pregnant despite all my inconveniences. When I was about 3 months pregnant, I went to church and asked for a prayer for the baby I was carrying inside. Pastor Eden of the People's Cathedral in Miami took me to her office and prayed. The baby jumped inside as soon as she put her hands on my belly as if he was listening to what she was praying for him. Glory to God! I used to go to church and sing; I could feel Jesse's little kicks inside like he was dancing. Wherever I went, I asked for prayers for us. I loved my baby, and despite the confusion and dysfunction in my home, I was grateful to have a child. I had a very difficult pregnancy, filled with abuse and sadness. I started searching for God more deeply, as I needed Him for myself and my baby. I had no one else, and my relationship with my husband was going downhill. When I was 28 weeks pregnant, we had a huge fight, and I left home to go to a friend's house. Early in the morning, I had a threat of miscarriage. I started bleeding, and the baby turned to the birthing position. He was only 28 weeks old. I asked different people for prayers when I was on my way to the hospital, and I was bleeding. I was in the hospital for a day. They gave me medication to strengthen my baby's lungs, and they put me on bed rest. Later, my baby was born 8 weeks early. Jesse weighed 5 pounds and was 7 inches long. The day Jesse was born, his father was crying. He had his son when he was 50, so it was a great day for him. Despite the hurtful words during my pregnancy, it was a good day for both of us. We took the baby home, and oh God, we were so happy. I had to wrap him in so many blankets; he was so small and fragile that he needed warmth and care. I believe God was training me for what was to come.

We brought Jesse home, and after a few hours, he was turning yellow. I put him in the sun, inside a small crib. After a few minutes, he cried out loud; the sun's rays were too hot for him, and he started crying frantically.

I picked it up and pushed the crib out of the sun quickly. On the third day of my baby being home, we took him back to the hospital. He was becoming more yellow, and we were worried. He was there for 3 days in an incubator. It was difficult for me to go to see him at the hospital and then go home alone. But every time we visited the hospital together, we fought on the way home. I felt depressed and anxious. The day came when, finally, my son Jesse was home forever; those were the longest 3 days for me. This little guy needed all my attention and care, so my focus was no longer on my husband nor trying to get from a man what only God could give me. Now Jesse needed my full attention. Little by little, I no longer expected the attention of a man; I turned my attention to a handsome boy who was stealing my heart and time. Surprisingly, my husband began to help me with him at night. He was in love with his son. He started sleeping with him and wanted to care for him, to the point that many times I thought he forgot that Jesse is also my son. For my husband, everything was his property: me, Jesse, his house, his jewelry, his money. I've always heard him say, "I have so much money, I have so much in jewelry." Jesse and I were owned by him as well. We presented Jesse to the Lord in church and always gave him our best. I knew the Lord had given me Jesse. God gave me his name when he was in my womb. In Hebrew, Jesse means: "God exists, God is real." My husband began to obsess over the child, even wanting to sleep with him alone in a room and take care of him; he was a very possessive man. Our relationship had improved, but the disrespect, the yelling, and the cursing continued in front of the boy. He disrespected and insulted me for anything, and I was reactive. Our relationship was turbulent and toxic, and the worst was in front of our son. We couldn't be together, but we couldn't be apart either. I left his side several times to find a place, mainly to my family in New York. But he called me and begged me to come back, and he even threatened me with the child. I liked for him to look for me, call me, and beg me to come back. I used to go home, and the same thing would happen after the honeymoon of the first few days was over. I remembered my mother's days when my father would come back after she had gone to her parents' house. They would come back together, and after a few days of honeymoon, repeatedly return to the same kind of abusive life.

Violence and abuse are a cycle; victims have to decide to get out of it and seek help. If not, it will continue to be repeated and become even worse. It takes courage and determination, but we also need help; we can't do it alone. But it can be done.

Miscarriages

Going back to my life in Miami, that's how my life was. I couldn't work because I was undocumented and didn't have a work permit, so my days were spent at home taking care of my son and working very hard to maintain our large, bright, and beautiful home. I got pregnant three times after my son Jesse was born and lost all three pregnancies involuntarily.

I was hoping for a brother or sister for Jesse. One of the miscarriages I had was at 28 weeks. I had very traumatic and sad experiences with each loss of a child. After Jesse was born, I had already bought all my baby's things; his room, his clothes, and everything he would need had been prepared. It was also a boy, but one day, my water broke. I called emergency services, and they took me to the hospital. The baby was born alive and very small. He had a breathing tube strapped to me. An hour later, the machine that was making the heartbeat noise horribly went beeeep... His little life was gone, and I, too, almost died after the birth of my child. My placenta didn't come out completely, the doctors suddenly left the room, and I was bleeding profusely. I felt my life go away from me. I yelled at my husband, who was the only one in the room with me, and I said, "I feel like I'm dying." he jumped out of the chair and yelled for the doctors and the nurses, who came into the room and helped me.

Losing my pregnancy was very painful and sad. I had postpartum depression, without the baby. I had extreme bleeding, and my breasts were leaking milk without a baby to breastfeed. What a horrible experience! When the baby's soul left, I saw my husband crying, asking God: Why, God, why? Interestingly, people don't take the Lord seriously, and then when something happens, we ask Him why. During that pregnancy, I had many people praying for me; I prayed too, and when this happened to me, I had many questions as well. However, some areas were not spiritually and emotionally healthy or aligned in my life. It was painful and shameful, and I felt guilty and desperate. I had severe postpartum depression.

Jesse started his life in a very dysfunctional house, hearing a lot of screaming and fighting, hearing his father denigrating his mother and seeing his mother not knowing what to do and responding with despair.

Screaming in a home is not pleasant and brings much pain and trauma to family members, especially children.

Today, I regret all my immaturity and disobedience. I let my hurts and feelings rule my life. I let myself be influenced so much by this man, and for a long time afterwards, I felt guilty for not standing firm and running away. I had no idea how to deal with my husband or what to do in my circumstances. I was afraid to seek help as an abused woman, but I didn't dare for fear of what would happen to me later when things got worse with my partner. But now I know better and can counsel other women and tell them: Get out and run for help!

My husband had all the characteristics of a narcissist, and it is not easy to get out of a relationship like that. I tell you that many do not understand, but it takes a lot for a woman to get up and seek help or get out of a toxic relationship.

Mostly, these types of men are looking for women who are empathetic and have family traumas from childhood, who have pain, insecurities, and various obvious needs in their souls.

I was a good candidate for a narcissist. After the loss of three pregnancies, I began to invest more and more of my time with Jesse. He was my company. Jesse and I used to go to church together, to the stores, to the parks, and now he was my center. Much of the time, we'd go to choir rehearsals together in church, and he'd go and try to play drums, as he was only three. He loved being with me. Since I was pregnant with him, I began to want more of God and to be different. I started serving in a new church, felt it was time to move to a new congregation and started attending Kendall's Jesus Christ Almighty Church, where I found beautiful people and also the pastors and friends who supported and accepted me.

My dad died

After I was in Miami, my dad and I would talk on the phone. I couldn't go to the Dominican Republic because I didn't have the necessary legal documents to come back. I would call him and tell him about Jesus as best I could. I still felt some fear deep down when I talked to him, but I thought that it was a time of healing and reconciliation. One day, he met my husband when I was deported for the first time, and he liked him. I guess they had a lot of things in common. "Joking'

Dad began to have many health problems. The doctor advised him to stop drinking alcohol and eat well, but he didn't. At the age of 66, he suffered a stroke and spent a few weeks in the hospital. I have peace of mind believing that my father received forgiveness for his sins while he was in the hospital. Many believers visited. I will forever love my father, and I know that, in his way, he loved me. I couldn't be at his funeral because, like I said, I was illegal in the United States, and my husband didn't want me to take my son with me to my home country because I most likely wouldn't be able to go back. I had to make the difficult decision not to go. It was an unfortunate day for me, the day my father died, and I couldn't go to his funeral. I felt locked up.

They told me that his funeral looked like someone very important had died. There was a line of people and vehicles at the funeral that took a long time to reach the house where he was being mourned. Amazingly, my father was loved by his friends and family. I have forgiven him, and I love my father to this day.

Chapter 10
Back behind bars

When Jesse was three and a half years old, I enrolled him in the pre-kindergarten program in a Christian school. I decided to go back to school to get a technical degree, which would give me a good job, I thought. I needed to do something with my life.

One morning in 1999, on my way to school, I was opening the gates that surrounded our luxurious house in Miami, when federal agents surrounded me. The officers asked me to confirm my name and the previous charges I had back in 1990. They told me that they were arresting me for re-entering the country after being deported. They mentioned the charges from 9 years ago, for which I had served a total of 5 years with outstanding behaviour. They entered my house, searched everywhere and interrogated me: who brought me, who helped me, and so on.

I prefer not to blame anyone; I realize that my decisions, my ambivalence, and lack of character led me to this point. I also didn't want to hurt the father of my youngest son; I had personal responsibility in this matter. They declared my rights, and it all felt like it was the first day when I was imprisoned years ago. I relived my imprisonment experience again. I was charged with the same crime I committed back in 1988. They handcuffed me, and we went to the nearest Federal Immigration Detention Center (immigration charges are federal charges).

On the way, I only thought about Jesse. He was three and a half years old and had just started attending his first school. This was difficult for him. He was adapting, but this experience distorted his life. Up until then, Jesse and I were inseparable. He had become my partner because we only had each other. His father worked in his jewelry store all day and often late into the night. We had a beautiful, big, expensive house, but he lacked the affection and time with his father, who used to come home after work, when Jesse was in bed. For my husband, his jewelry business and making money were his life; he always boasted about his money. He had just bought some nice furniture for the house and had paid the rest of what we owed for the big home.

He had bought that house at a reasonable price. This huge house had everything, materially speaking, a pool, a patio, a huge jacuzzi, marble floors and more, but we lacked the real thing; we lacked a home made up of a real family.

No one visited me, and my family was in another country. My husband did not like to interact with other people. So I lived alone with Jesse, but what the family needed was a home. There is a difference between a house and a real home. Before leaving the house that day with the agents, I was able to call my husband and tell him that I was detained for re-entering the country. When I talked to him, his voice broke down in tears. I told him to pick Jesse up from school and asked him to arrange for a caregiver for our son at home. Once again, my world collapsed. Before my arrest, life had begun to settle. I was firmly serving God in my local church, and I felt that I was changing. I could change my partner, or at least God would, that was my faith, or my presumption, I should say.

There is a difference between faith and presumption.

Before I was arrested (when Jesse was about a year old), we started to get along better. We were more stable without fighting as much. I prayed for my partner. We both needed deliverance and inner healing. I was serving in the church; I was always asking God to change him. I don't remember praying to the Lord to change me; I also needed changes in my life.

Now, I understand that change must start with me.

God allows situations to transform us internally. Because He is interested in forming Himself in us and showing His glory, He will also enable circumstances for us to set some boundaries and grow up. Christian character is formed within us as we go through life's challenges and difficulties. We need to yield to the Lord to break the bondage that our sins and rebellions have caused to our souls, and we do not want to give up.

I complained incessantly about my husband and agonized, wanting him to change. I asked my church family for prayer as I told them about my situation.

I remember, I used to tell this sister in Christ the whole story, what he was doing to me, how he was treating me and so on. This lady, I suppose, was tired of hearing the same thing. She once suggested to me, "Joselyn, why don't you use everything that's going on between you and your husband, all your afflictions, as stepping stones to lift yourself higher and grow more in God?" I never understood what this dear sister was saying to me at the time, but now I do.

The different situations, struggles and challenges that happen to us can be due to many reasons. Due to our choices, rebellion, lack of faith, lack of surrender, lack of knowledge, fear, disobedience, or so many other reasons, but when we belong to God, we go through inner processes, and that will form in us His character.

When we bring our afflictions to the cross and die to ourselves, it brings us closer to Christ and transforms our lives. Most of the time, we will go through a revolving door, and it takes time until we bend, yield, and learn.

I also remember the words of someone close to me: "Joselyn, I have been praying and fasting for you, and the Lord wants you to die." I got the message.

Die to myself. Our fleshly nature, ego, and mindset get us into a lot of trouble, but the Lord wants us to live through the Spirit, not the flesh. In my case, despite everything, I insisted that my husband go to church with me. I focused on changing him and helping him become a good Christian. From time to time, he would go reluctantly. Other times, I went to church with Jesse, but he stayed home. When Jesse and I got home, he made sure to make my life miserable, starting a big fight, igniting his anger and cursing me with some Cuban names that degraded me.

Some days, I used to come from church and put up with all the bad words he could say to me. I used to ask the Lord to help me ignore him and not get into an argument with him. I pleaded with my heavenly Father on the way home from church, "Lord, help me to control myself and not respond to him, don't let his words hurt me, and let me be quiet."

But there were also other days when, even though I prayed on the way home, there was so much emotional pressure and yelling. When I arrived, I would get into an argument with him, and I would lose the peace and joy I had brought from church. The church was a source of peace for me because at home, I had none. We both needed help. There came a time when I recognized my deep needs, but my husband thought he was perfect. I have many other anecdotes, and many times I wanted to throw in the towel. But, somehow, I managed to stay. At the time I am writing, he has been dead for a few years. I hope that God, in His mercy, in his last moments, had compassion on him, and that he was able, during his days in the hospital, to sincerely cry out to the Lord from his spirit, because of all those prayers and tears that I and many others had raised to the Lord for him over many years. He died of a stroke, but he had the opportunity to spend a week in a hospital. During that time, I was praying for him, from where I was in my country, so that the Lord would give him a chance in His Kingdom. I think in his last moment, within his spirit, he repented and received Jesus into his heart.

Going back to 1999. Immigration picked me up at my home in Miami. They took me to a federal detention. I could only imagine Jesse's little face when he couldn't find his mother. I was supposed to pick him up from school at noon. My arrest happened around ten in the morning. I was broken and inconsolable, very fearful and worried. What's going to happen to me? And Jesse? Who could take care of him? My husband was sad and cornered too; life had hit us both on many occasions, and this was one of them again. In any case, I, too, had disobeyed God by deciding to return illegally to the United States and by not trusting and surrendering to the Lord. I should have been open to let God do His perfect will in my life, but I was very stubborn. So much guilt was now haunting me.

When I arrived at the holding cell, I saw a scene similar to one I had experienced years earlier. Maybe it was even more painful now because I was leaving behind my son, who was used to me, with a father who might almost be his grandfather and didn't know much about caring for a child. My husband was hurt twice as much because he discovered that one of his daughters had called immigration to report that I had entered, and I was in the country illegally. When I arrived at the detention center, they began the procedures to let me in. I started to pray and cry.

Oh, Lord, how sorry I was that I decided to return illegally to the United States. How many wrong decisions had I made in my life that robbed me of God's best. And now it was significantly affecting my beloved little boy.

The following days began the judicial sessions, interrogation, and once again, I decided to keep the details secret and cover up for my partner. In this case, the father of my youngest son paid to bring me back. I thought that if I said that he had paid, he would also have to face charges, and our son Jesse would be left with no one outside prison. Anyway, it was my decision, and I had my part in it. I started, from inside prison, to try to find someone to help us with Jesse because his father was very limited in his relationships with people. He didn't trust anyone, he didn't have any real friends, and he didn't have anyone he trusted enough to enter his house, as he was very suspicious.

Jesse went from one house to another as if he were without a family because his father had to work. Although he was the business owner, he did not allow himself extra time off to attend to his son's needs. He never found a suitable person to take care of our son in his own home. He was a complicated man to understand, with a strong spirit of rejection, and therefore, he excelled in business and had a lot of money. He was proud of his possessions, which showed on the surface, but he was insecure and harboured many negative emotions from his childhood. We both carried great strongholds and traumas in our lives.

I never understood him. The people around him didn't want to associate with him except for business. As I said, I did the unspeakable to see if I could help him, trying to change him. Still, I ended up sinking like him into anger, sadness, agony, and frustration, without any solution, and sometimes even despair. But this time, the pain went beyond the problems between the two of us. Now we were divided for the second time and possibly for a long time, because I was in prison, this time with federal charges. I talked to people outside to see if they could help with Jesse, and I offered to pay. People in the church tried to help for a while, but the biggest challenge was dealing with the controversial personality of my son's father.

Jesse needed his mother, father, and God's protection, but instead, he went to one house today and tomorrow to the other, so he grew up in a variety of homes. I was told that he was always looking out the window, waiting for his mother to come and pick him up. Wherever he stayed, he was always asking where his mother was. "Where's Mommy? Where is Mommy!?" God only knows the pain I felt when I was forced to leave my son without anyone's help. It is still difficult to imagine the sadness and loneliness of my helpless son and his father, not knowing what to do and having to deal with his pain and frustration. I was told that Jesse was asking Papa God to bring his mom back to him. On one occasion, the prison visit was cancelled, and they didn't let Jesse see me. His father was with him; his screaming could be heard in the hallways. They told me he was crying, asking to see his mother. When he came to see me, all the time, he went home crying and cursing at the officers who had me locked up (that's how he saw it), screaming to them to let his mommy go. Of all my pains, this has been the greatest, leaving my youngest son alone with his father. I carried great pain, remorse, condemnation, guilt and sadness for having done things my way; it hurt so much that I felt myself dying inside.

Again, in a courtroom

The day of court came, and there wasn't much anyone could do to support me. I re-entered the country illegally; there is not much justification for that. Anyway, I asked for mercy, for myself and the sake of my son. I apologized to the court. I acknowledged my mistakes in court. How stubborn and foolish I had been; my son could have been born in Santo Domingo when I was deported, and we could have been together. Many things were going through my mind. How much damage I had done to my son, my partner at the time, and myself by doing things my way and for not standing my ground and saying I'm not going back! My codependency on a man was greater at that time than my convictions. I was so stubborn. Again, in that courtroom, I saw the atmosphere that was already familiar to me, and I could feel the fear in my heart with chills in the pit of my stomach and sadness. It is an inexplicable feeling and emotion that only God and I know. The day of the court arrived; they chained my hands to my waist and ankles with a padlock. I went out to any outside appointments in chains. In the institutions, they searched us when we were about to leave and when we returned. They took us in chains everywhere, most of the time with officers who made you feel less than nothing because of their position of authority. However, not all officers were the same; there were also compassionate ones.

By the day of my federal court appearance, many people from my church came to support me. The court guards looked a little worried. Those people went to the section to support me, and they even wrote a letter and collected signatures to show me their support. I used to serve and help the church, despite my anguish at home and within. I always loved serving and helping others. The people from the Jesus Christ Almighty Church in Kendall, Miami, and others outside the church offered support because they knew my heart and my love for people and God, but none of that helped in the court decision. I am grateful to this day for their support. They were trying to show the fact that I wasn't innocent of re-entering illegally, but I was someone different in the way I lived, and they had also seen me walk and what I was like. The pastor, his wife, and a few others had known me personally for a couple of years. When I was in front of the judge, I asked for forgiveness from the court and had all these people supporting me. Since I came back to the United States, I have not been involved in any legal problems or criminal activity. But none of that had any good effect on the heart of the immigration judge, and I was given a 46-month sentence in a federal institution.

Along with the sentence, it was added that once the federal sentence was over, I had to go and serve the remainder of my original State sentence. Reader, do you remember that I was released from prison earlier through a commutation of sentence? I had a conditional pardon. I still needed to go back to another section of the court to handle this.

My son became more violent and cried every day. His father had enough money to find someone responsible to take care of our son in his home, but he decided not to. Jesse needed a home and a caregiver. It was a challenge to deal with and help a child with so much pain in his little heart. The only thing his father did was yell at him and punish him. His father was also dealing with his pain, in addition to all the baggage he brought generationally. Someone told me that he used to lock Jesse in a dark room in the house when the boy didn't want to eat or was rebellious. God only knows how Jesse felt and what that child went through. As I learned, Jesse would cry in that dark room, and his father would let him cry for hours. On my court day, I was sentenced to 46 months in a federal institution and sent to prison 480 miles away, driving almost 7 hours from Miami to Tallahassee, the capital of Florida.

God's Intervention

Luis used to visit me with Jesse. They stayed in a hotel. The visits were now about every month. Once, after closing the jewelry store, my husband decided to go out to see me at night with Jesse, and they had an accident.

They crashed down a ravine, and the car in which they were travelling was a total loss. The vehicle rolled down a hill and into a large tree below. Jesse flew out of the car, and my husband was cornered inside the vehicle. Only God protected them. That's all I can say. Someone saw them going down the hill on the freeway, and they called 911. The police rescued them, took them to the hospital and then helped them find a rental car. My husband didn't want to stay in the hospital, but he wanted to see me and not miss the visit that weekend, so he took a rental car and arrived at the prison with some minor wounds on his head and pain in his body. Jesse was unharmed. Luis told me that when the police helped them, they were signalling to Jesse, saying, "A miracle." The angels protected you, and they smiled at him. My God, thank you for these and so many mercies for me and my family. They arrived the next day to visit me, with their heads full of shards of glass and residue in their hair.

I spent four years in federal prison. These years were even more complex than the previous ones in the state institution because now I was not only imprisoned with my memories and my attachment to a man who was my husband, but now, I had the pain of a mother who left her young son without help. I turned to God again with a broken heart. This time was excruciating, even more lonely and devastating. I did not stop thinking about my son. I did everything I could from the inside. I asked for forgiveness and help from within the institution, trying to shorten my time and hoping that the United States of America would have mercy on my son, without any success. I wrote to the senators, and I even wrote to the president asking for forgiveness and help, but I felt as if I had been buried alive. Most of us prisoners call, and no one listens to us. We are distressed and struggle to be alive, but we run out of strength to be able to scream because we are marginalized in society, and no one believes in us. I know that there is a lot of guilt within prisons, crimes and a lot of evil, but I also know that there are people in there who are not perfect or innocent but who regret what they have done and want a new and different life. There are many inside who are guilty, but sometimes the real and biggest culprits are out there having a great life, especially in the drug business. I do not excuse our wrongdoings, but it's true.

I also know from experience that if a prisoner turns to the Lord with sincere faith, their life can be truly transformed, and when they come out, they can be a productive and fruitful individual if true repentance has taken place in their life. I am a witness to God's power in prison. Some are freer there than many who are outside. But sin is sin, guilt is guilt, and evil and wrongdoing and wrong choices have consequences. In my case, I am a child of God, and the Lord Himself allowed all of this; my decisions and stubbornness led to significant consequences. My heart had to be healed and set free, and I wouldn't let the Lord do it at that time.

I wasn't aware of inner healing and deliverance; at least, I hadn't received the teaching or revelation about it. Most churches do not teach about it.

I didn't know that God wanted to form His character in me. He wanted me to speak and do things for Him, but His desire and plan for me is to know Him and for me to receive His love. I am his daughter, but at that time, I had not yet fully realized my identity.

To be a Christian is to be a true child of Christ, to have a relationship with our Father, to know who we are and to live a life that reflects His character of love, the fruit of the Spirit, peace, holiness, faith, consecration, surrender, humility, and much more. It may sound too much to some, but through the Holy Spirit, we can; He helps us in our weaknesses.

I have learned that every man and woman of God will go through processes of "afflictions" for God's character to be formed in us, because man alone in his humanity cannot manifest God. Those who walk in the flesh do not glorify God. That which is of the Spirit gives us life, and all that is of the flesh and disobedience brings death. The Lord teaches us discipline, but we need to be teachable, be willing to receive, and be humble.

I served my forty-six-month sentence for illegally re-entering the United States.

Chapter 11
I left the Feds behind

The day of leaving that prison arrived. Once again, I needed to prepare myself mentally and emotionally. Immigration would come looking for me for deportation, but I still had to face charges in the state institution for having violated the conditions of the commutation of the sentence in 1994. It was the year 2003. Immigration came to pick me up at the federal prison and took me to the Florida State Jail. Once again, I was chained and transferred to a state penitentiary. The living conditions in the state institutions are much worse than the federal ones, with fewer resources and more hostility. I spent a few long months again waiting for the state court sessions. I needed to face a judge for the rest of the state time I owed since 1994.

My husband got me a lawyer to help me in court. When the time came for the court section, the attorney made a motion to go alone without me. I didn't have to be present. I also had uncertainty while I waited. Could it be that I will have to do that remaining time? I asked myself inside. I still owed almost four years to the State of Florida. The judge granted me time served, which was a relief. I waited a few more months, going from place to place to get to where Immigration would pick me up and send me back to the Dominican Republic.

Let my son go with me

Before I left the United States, I begged my husband to let Jesse go with me to my country. I am his mother, and I was willing to be the mother he needed me to be. Jesse is American, and I needed his father's permission to take him to the Dominican Republic with me. I knew I was going to be deported for many years this time. But there was no way to convince my husband or make him understand. I begged him for my son, but nothing changed his mind. He wanted to keep our son; he said Jesse was his companion, and he would be better off with him. He had the money to take care of Jesse and everything he needed.

He didn't think about the child or me; He was thinking about himself and how he would feel if the child went away with me, even though he was neither emotionally nor physically capable of being a good father. I was depressed and sad because now I was leaving my son in a distant country, and the sentence and punishment according to immigration would be 20 years before I could apply for permission to re-enter, that is, if I was accepted again.

The night before I departed for my country, my ex-husband came to visit me. I was in a detention center, in transition to my final place, where I was going to be deported. He took Jesse to see me. That night, I cried uncontrollably. I asked him again to let me take our son to the Dominican Republic. I saw Jesse's tears fall from his sad, small face; it broke my heart. He couldn't say anything because he was afraid of his father. Jesse was 8 years old at the time. We talked through a thick glass window. On one side, I, and on the other, my son and his father, without physical contact. That was the rule of that specific prison. I couldn't hug him. He raised his little right hand, touching the glass. I did the same on the other side, and we felt our hands imaginatively. In my heart, it was a lot for me. This was also torture for my soul. I left the United States with the warning that I couldn't return. After so many years, I could apply, but there was no promise it would be accepted. I left behind so many dreams, so many good and bad experiences, and the most precious thing to me, my little son, and the man I married. I had so many questions in my mind.

I arrived in the Dominican Republic. I was at the same port of entry as I was several years ago, but this time it was a little different. I was greeted by 3 of my blood sisters. The re-entry process and my departure from the immigration offices and the police department were shorter. In my country and culture, you must have influential relationships to facilitate most of what you need. Someone in the family was a high-ranking officer of the Army who encouraged and helped me with everything concerning my arrival. One of my sisters, my dear Rita, took me to her house and offered me what little she had. I lived there for a few months. I kept depending on my husband for everything. I called him several times a day because I wanted to live my life and his life too, and he was also the same. My husband continued to control and manipulate me from a distance, this time even using my son. After a few months of living with my sister, I moved into a rented apartment on my own. I asked my ex-husband to help me have my own space, and he reluctantly helped me. It was his duty as a husband, but with him, I had to beg him for everything. I also begged him to send my son to see me personally.

Jesse finally came to visit me!

I wanted so much to share time with Jesse. Time passed, and finally, after almost a year, I was able to spend time with him. We were happy. It was a great blessing for me to spend time not only with Jesse but also with my first son in my home country. Aneurys shared time with his brother for the first time. What a blessing it was to me.

I started working as I needed to be free and to break away from the great codependency I had with my husband. Even though I had a deep desire to get closer to God, I felt that I was linked to so many things, and I felt like I was in a hole that I couldn't get out of on my own. I didn't know how to let the Holy Spirit work in me as there were horrible and strong strengths and bonds, which I couldn't understand or explain. I was dragging a cart full of emotional luggage. It seemed to me that I could not see the light. There was constant suffering, attachment to people, wrong decisions, making mistakes, and even hurting others. I didn't know how to get rid of it. I felt like I was getting into the mud most of the time and spreading it everywhere I went. That's how I looked and felt. At that time, I did not know what codependency and rejection were. I also harboured a lack of forgiveness, even if I said with my mouth that I forgave. I didn't understand everything that was affecting me; I couldn't put a name to it. Sometimes, I thought that was life. I slowly learned about trauma, codependency, inner healing, and deliverance. I needed to work on myself and let the Spirit of God work in me. In other words: Let go, Joselyn !

Surrender? Yes, surrender brings pain. For many of us, our souls and minds are defective, bound and wounded, and we must renew and surrender them every day. Take it one day at a time.

I will make you understand, and I will teach you how you should walk; I will fix my eyes on you. Do not be like the horse, or like the mule, without understanding who is to be fastened with a halter and a bridle, because if not, they don't come near you.

(Psalm 32:8-9)

That verse of the Word of the Lord is powerful. I always tried to yield, give up, and surrender completely to the Lord. I had a sincere intention to do so, but when the pain began to pull me in many ways, with wrong thoughts, traumas, pain, stubbornness, and actions, I would come back to occupy the throne of my life. Then, I would regret it, repent once and then I would start acting again as I did not know the Lord. I was like the Israelites when God brought them out of Egypt and Moses led them. They complained, displayed bad attitudes, sinned against God, and chose to disobey and worship idols. The consequences were devastating, causing them to go in circles. It took them 40 years of a journey that was allotted for only a few days to reach the Promised Land. That was also a reality for me. I don't know about you, dear reader, but I, unfortunately, had to learn many of life's lessons in my youth days through the consequences of my actions, due to my decisions, stubbornness, and having an ill soul. It took me much longer to learn the lessons to move forward at different stages of life.

If we are going round and round in the same circumstances, it is wise to stop and ask ourselves: Why is this happening, and why do we find ourselves in the same or similar situations? What do I need to learn, change, or obey here?

Thank God for those of you who have been teachable and most likely obedient since you received the Lord, or at least you weren't as stubborn as I was. I had problems. When I returned to my home country, I was married, with a long-distance relationship, if we can even call it a marriage. I was back in my beautiful tropical country, the Dominican Republic, and my ex-husband was in the United States. Our son was caught between us, living with his father but wanting to be with his mother. I longed to have my son and for my marriage to work, but apparently, my ex-husband didn't do much to make the relationship work. He had a reasonable sum of money in the banks of the Dominican Republic, and once a year, he came to visit me. His attitude went like this: You're my wife on paper, but I'm the one who makes the rules of the game. I'm rich, and you need me. Our relationship was frayed. I didn't know what else to do. I tried every means I could to convince him to visit the Dominican Republic more often or move to my country. Perhaps he could buy an apartment or visit here every few months. He had the money and could do that and more. He could do so if he wanted our relationship to work, but that was not what he wanted. It was a very difficult situation. I was daydreaming, and I wasn't realistic.

My husband left after visiting me for the first time. He phoned me, and although we talked, he never believed me or trusted me. I think he was judging me for this condition. He always said: "Love from afar, love of losers" (I'm not sure I understand this term). He never did anything to stay close. Therefore, I received abuse and manipulation, even from a distance. When he came to visit me, I felt as if I was just another object of his and not a wife. The situation was not strange to me, as I felt that way most of the time in that relationship. I could feel the sarcasm, intrigue, and manipulation because I needed him financially, given my mindset and insecurities at the time. He felt superior because he was rich, and I was poor. I felt so much emptiness in my life. I didn't have a true revelation of who I was in Christ. He lived as the prodigal son in the Bible. I was tired of being controlled and threatened over the phone, manipulated emotionally, often reminded of my obligations to him, shouted at with profanity and denigrating words, falsely accused and subjected to outbursts of anger. I was tired of waiting for him to visit. We had so many arguments and conflicts that my life had deteriorated even more. My whole family knew about our dilemma and knew how conflicted I was. They couldn't understand why I was attached to this man.

I had to seek psychological and emotional help from the Department of Domestic Violence and Abuse in my country. I started thinking about getting a divorce. I even consulted some of God's people. Even though they knew the circumstances, they told me not to get a divorce. I convinced myself that it was better to divorce him because he wouldn't change, and he wouldn't come to live with me in the DR. I always prayed and asked other Christians to pray for our relationship. I sincerely believed that he would change his life, that he would truly give himself to Christ, and that our marriage would be different. One day, I picked up the courage and found a good, reputable lawyer. I had no money, but this lawyer worked on commissions. He knew, from what I told him, that my husband was a rich man. I filed for divorce, and they seized all the money from his bank in the DR. The lawyer also worked to seize his money in the United States, where my husband had his big business. When the lawyers notified my husband about the lawsuit, a massive war began. He got angry and began to threaten to kill me for what I had done. After a few days, he changed and began to behave like a dove, crying, promising all kinds of good things and saying that he was going to change. He promised to come and visit me more often, to work, to be better for our family, to allow Jesse to be with me, and to buy me a lovely apartment. He told me he didn't want a divorce, begged me, and told me he couldn't live without me.

For days, I stood firm in my decision. My lawyer was sure that my husband would have to pay me half of his properties and allow Jesse to be with me. I was relieved to know that I could be free and move on with my life, even though I was sad deep down, because I didn't know if I was doing the right thing. I thought, I'm a Christian, could it be that I am disobeying God by demanding a divorce? Is this what God wants for my life? I was overwhelmed with so many thoughts.

Victim of rejection

My ex-husband used to phone me a couple of times every day. He sent me flowers and gifts from Miami. He even called the pastor of the church I was going to in Santo Domingo and made a generous donation to them. He told the pastor that he loved me, that divorce was not God's will, and that we should fight for the sake of our marriage. He asked the pastor to talk to me and counsel me because we have a son, and God's will for our marriage is to stay together. I assure you, dear reader, that he suddenly became a very splendid and kind man. He transformed himself into another man. He came to visit me and convinced me to remove the divorce proceedings and relinquish control of his money in the bank. Despite my disbelief in him and several pieces of advice from others close to me, I went to the lawyer and asked him to withdraw the divorce suit. I told him I didn't want to get divorced anymore. The lawyer got angry and said to me in front of my husband, "This one came to deceive you, Joselyn; he's just using you, and you're going to see it!"

I didn't listen to the lawyer or the red flag inside of me, and I dropped the divorce suit. My husband took me to the bank, and I removed the hold on our money. After he left for Miami, I went to withdraw cash from the bank account. I discovered that no more than a few pesos were left in the bank account. The man had taken everything out of the bank, and then he called me and said, "I don't forgive you for what you did to me. Do you think I went there for you? I went to get my money." Feeling betrayed and disappointed and not knowing how to deal with so much inner pain, I felt denigrated. I became bitter and depressed. I even stopped serving in the church. I was angry and disappointed with God, with me, and with my ex-husband. At the time, I was attending a church, but I wasn't receiving much spiritually because of my condition. I needed deliverance and renewal of my mind in the Word so badly. The pain led me to resentment and complaining. I did not submit to God nor my spiritual authorities. For a long time, I did not know how to let God work and let go. Little by little and more and more deeply, I fell apart and continued to make decisions that brought me serious consequences. My soul was in conflict and dealing with many external and internal problems. So, after all this, my ex-husband found a well-paid lawyer in the United States and filed for divorce in Miami, unbeknownst to me. The lawyer sent a letter to the wrong address in the Dominican Republic, deliberately, citing me for the divorce in Florida. The letter was returned because I did not reside at that address. The lawyer orchestrated the situation to say to the court that my husband did not know where I was and that he had not communicated with me since I was released from prison. This was a big lie. The lawyer managed to divorce us without my knowledge, and my ex kept everything, including custody of my son Jesse, which was a significant loss for me. I didn't find out until two years later that I was already divorced. The divorce was in

2005, and I found out in 2007. It was devastating because, in my mind and at the bottom of my heart, I didn't want the marriage to end. I always believed that God would change him, that we would be together again, and that things would be different.

This behaviour is typical of abused women; we are insecure and full of rejection, and we always hope that the man, no matter how narcissistic he is, and no matter how toxic our relationship is, we are convinced Things will change if we act in a particular way; according to us, our partner will change; we live in denial.

We say, "God can change him if I believe and pray more, or submit to him more, everything will be fine." That is far from the truth. We use every excuse we can to wait and wait, hang in there and hold on, while our partner doesn't give a thought about what we feel. They continue to control and denigrate us to feel superior to us. Their inferiority is projected as superiority. It's complex, but now I understand it. The woman who suffers abuse and violence is always blaming herself and questioning everything.

If you are being abused or manipulated, seek help. You can do it. You are stronger than you think.

Chapter 12

I Must Get Back Up Again

Finally, after learning of the divorce and much humiliation, I picked up the courage to decide not to welcome that man back into my life. He was having adventures with all kinds of women in Miami. Naïve as I was, I had believed that our marriage would somehow work and get better. I think, deep down, that I filed for divorce mainly to get his attention and not to divorce. During all those 15 years of marriage, I believed, prayed, and hoped that things would be different. Neither he nor I ever surrendered to the Lord, nor did we seek the right help. My ex never believed in seeking help or advice. I was always focused on him in my codependency, and tried to help him, instead of focusing on myself, seeking help, and facing what needed to be dealt with inside of me to have a better life.

But yes, again, I decided to get up. This time, I decided to keep going; that voice inside me kept lifting me and wouldn't let me stay on the ground.

A hurt, emotionally and mentally ill person is not fit to start a new relationship after a divorce. We need to heal and release all the old baggage that we bring, and this takes time. So we need patience and courage to wait to be healed. The process is not pleasant, but with the Holy Spirit, we can go through it.

At the time I write, I already understand, but before that, it was tough for me to disassociate myself from toxic relationships. Spiritually, I tried to seek God and do His will, but I wouldn't give up. Like many, I preached, prayed, and served in the church. I have always had a heart to serve, to help others, and to give, but I did not let the Spirit of the Lord tame me. In other words, I did know what to do, but I usually went and did the opposite of what I had learned or understood was God's will. I was a carnal and emotional Christian.

The Lord was so good that, even in my follies and bad decisions, He kept sending me help, giving me dreams, visions, and showing His Word, His work of love for me.

I have paid a great price for my stubbornness but thank the Father for His mercy and faithfulness to me and my loved ones today. For you, my reader. He loves you and cares for you.

Today, I can write about this from a different side just because of God's mercy, grace, love, and power.

"I will shape you through the process."—God.

"Behold, like the clay in the potter's hand, so are you in My hand, O house of Israel." (Jeremiah 18:6b)

I can't believe now how stupid, blind, fearful, and codependent I was. My Lord! I was sick. The polishing and pruning process IS NECESSARY. I had lost everything, rejected by the man I wanted to keep at all costs. Now, I was in my home country, with nothing and no one to naturally depend on, trying to have a healthy life and find peace. Little by little, all the natural things on which I depended faded away. I couldn't have my son with me, no matter how hard I tried to get help to claim him from the United States. I made all kinds of requests and petitions in different family and children agencies in the Dominican Republic. I tried to get help to have Jesse in my country, but his father, a U.S. citizen, had full custody after the divorce. He had the last word in our son's life, and I was at his mercy to let my son travel to visit me and share time with me. I cried so many times, for all my mistakes and my children. The guilt was tremendous in my heart for Jesse's outcome, and for not being able to raise my firstborn, Aneurys. I began to have deep economic needs. What little I had, I lost. I sold it to survive, and

I lived from one house to another until I had nothing more to sell. I had to sell an apartment that I owned, a car, furniture and everything. I found myself with absolutely nothing, and not many people around me were willing to help. I felt ashamed, despised and alone.

Only the hand of the Lord and His love were with me. He was there through human instruments that He used to help me from time to time. His Spirit—despite my struggles, ugliness, and confusion—was there with me, even when the pain was so great that I sometimes did not recognize His presence. I had no natural hope and was mocked by the enemy. One morning, I heard the loud laughter of the enemy, and with that sound, I suddenly woke up. I realized that I had been very foolish, stubborn, and rebellious, with resentment even against God, even though I called on His name and prayed. I didn't give up completely, but my soul resisted everything. I used to feel that little inner voice that said, "Forgive and let go," but I didn't know how to, or sometimes I didn't want to let go. I convinced myself I had forgiven, but the wounds hadn't healed. I was full of faults, offences, ambitions, and even greed. So, God allowed me to go into the wilderness and endure dry times. It was difficult to break free from so many bonds. It was a real breakdown, like olives that are crushed to produce oil.

At first, I didn't even know what the word "process" was. I was afraid of that word. It was terrifying to me. I thought, "How is it that a good God allows me to be suffering and go through all this in life? Something is wrong that I don't understand." I blamed others, myself, or the devil. I didn't ask for the process, and I didn't want it either, but I guess God knew what was best for me. Smile. Oh, Lord, how I needed to go through the crushing process, and I didn't realize or admit it. I lived in denial, with a great spirit of being a victim and constantly crying, "poor me."

Over time, I learned that much is also demanded of those who are given a lot in the Kingdom.

"To whom much is given, much is required." (Luke 12:48)

That means people are accountable for what they have been given.

I learned that I am spirit, soul, and body. My spirit becomes one with Him when I receive Jesus and invite Him to come into my heart and give Him my life, but there is a soul and a mind that need to be renewed and given to Him. As Romans 12:1-2 says, we need to be renewed in our minds and not conform to this world. (paraphrased) We cannot live between two waters as Christians; it is very dangerous.

The spirit and the flesh are opposed, and there is an internal war in which we have no peace and tranquillity. The whole process is agonizing, painful, and challenging because, in the process, we lose everything. God loves us all. The Lord desires the self, ego, and the flesh to die in us if He is to be truly glorified in our lives. There is a pull between our soul and our spirit when we do not give up and let God work. It is very uncomfortable and painful. God wants us to be truly free.

When we don't surrender, we're not happy with God, but we're not satisfied in the world either. The Bible tells us: You will know the Truth, and the Truth will set you free. (John 8:31) And to that truth that we know, we have to add faith and obedience.

Crossing the sea in 2010

Someone invited me to a particular church. I went to visit that apostolic, prophetic church, Monte de Dios Church in Santo Domingo, where I had to start over. There, I began to learn about the condition of my soul and the need to surrender completely. I began to know and understand inner healing, deliverance, surrender, and doing things God's way. To walk in obedience and justice. I began to learn about the doors we open that the enemy uses to deceive and defeat us. It was a church where prayer, God's Word, and equipping God's children in spiritual warfare were the backbone of ministry. The pastors are people who lived what they preached and loved the Lord. For me, that church was a spiritual training ground. I learned to be naked in God's presence, being honest and confronting all those areas that I needed to confront in my life and receive deliverance and healing by being honest with myself. I learned and sought help the right way. I began to look at myself in the mirror of God's Word through His Holy Spirit. I was set free from self-condemnation and guilt, I also stopped blaming others, and I was free from the spirit of being a victim and self-sabotage. It wasn't easy at first, but I began to understand the condition I was in and how shameful it was to have lived so wrongly in my attempt to walk and serve God on my terms. I began to have intimate and sincere communion with God. I had no choice if I wanted to live and get out of all the mud I was in.

I admitted my sin, my iniquities, and my own wrong decisions. I had nowhere to turn, no man, no money, no work, and very few friends. Sometimes, the people I thought I was closest to became distant, not because they didn't want to help, but because God, my Father, allowed it. I didn't have a job, nor could I find one. I began to receive revelation about how carnal I was and about Jesus' unconditional love for me. He loves me so much that He couldn't leave me unchanged.

The *Lord accepts us as we are, but He loves us so much that He wouldn't leave us the same.*

I began to understand the need for inner healing and deliverance and became willing to receive it. I began to realize that my worst enemy was neither the devil, people, nor the world; it was myself, because I did not have a renewed mind and a regenerated soul. I began to confront myself alone and not blame anyone else. I had a revelation and conviction that I had a lack of forgiveness, resentment, doubt, rejection, a victim's spirit, fear, anger, control, and pride, affecting my life. I began to surrender it to God to the best of my ability, to live the Word of God, the truth that He teaches us through the Bible. I have freed myself from that spirit of double mentality, from being good with God one day and resentful and complaining the next. I often damaged everything with my attitude and my words, always doing what I wanted to do. Emotions and our own decisions drive most Christians. Even today, I must be careful and submit to God every day. He is not done with us yet; we are far from it.

But He who began the good work in us will complete it.

"Assuring of this very thing, He who began a good work in you will complete it until the day of Jesus Christ." *(Philippians 1:6)*

I thank the Lord for the people who teach us not only one side of the gospel or a beautiful preaching that thrills us but teach us how to put God's truth into practice and to obey to be blessed and healed. I thank the Lord for mentors who confront us with reality, in the love of God and with a genuine interest in helping us. Others discourage you, condemn you, criticize you, and judge you, even in our Christian circle. But those things won't harm us if we know our identity in Christ and choose to walk in love.

I thank God for finding good teachers, intercession, and support. God uses His people as vessels of honour to help and edify us. It was in that moment that I gained a deeper understanding of myself and had a revelation of how my spirit, soul, and body intertwine to glorify God when I surrender and practice what He teaches me. However, if one of the areas is not aligned, subdued, and renewed, it causes a division within. Thank the Lord also for the people who invest their time in us and teach us to love the Lord and to be honest with God, to recognize our vulnerability. No one is perfect, but there is honour in acknowledging our weaknesses, vulnerabilities, sins, and wrongdoings.

Again, I am thankful for all the people God has used to pray for me, counsel me, and give me, by grace, what they have received by grace. I learned to free my soul, to open it, to prepare myself to be healthy and truly free. I knew the need to have only one mind, despite what I feel or see with my natural eyes.

Double mentality is killing the faith and courage of God's people; it is a tactic that the enemy uses to distract us and make us fall into discouragement and rebellion. We need to maintain the focus without going backwards. Double-minded people accomplish nothing with God, as He says in James 4:8: *"Draw near to God and He will draw near to you. Sinners, clean your hands; and you who are double-minded, purify your hearts."* Here, He makes us understand that people with a double mentality are not pure. The Bible instructs us to purify our hearts, and that only happens with God's Word, yielding, and obeying.

I learned to resist and renounce fear, duality, laziness, rejection, insecurities, pride, vainglory, depression, despair, and anxiety, and to receive healing for all the pain and trauma. Although life may be a long journey, we can be healed and free from generational iniquities and sin by accepting what Jesus Christ did on the Cross.

We can manage our inner struggles and be free from our conflicts when we let the Holy Spirit work in us. I used to self-sabotage everything, but the Lord has changed and continues to change my heart. I realized that I had to stop blaming others for my actions and take responsibility for my disobedience and stubbornness. I recognized that I needed a transformation in my life, and that would only happen when I died to myself, in my ways and carnalities. I hit rock bottom spiritually. My life was a disaster; I took two steps forward and four steps back. I had to repent, not just with lip service, but from deep within. The Holy Spirit now gave me conviction, and I was sensitive to Him. I repented and renounced everything that He brought to my heart and mind. I asked the Lord for forgiveness with tears and brokenness from the depths of my being. The Father loves me, but He has had to deal significantly with my heart and my attitudes. I had to choose to go back to my first love and let the Lord Jesus Christ be Lord in my life. I needed to let God truly reveal Himself in my soul and actions and love Him more than anything else for who He is, and not for what I want from Him or for my ideas and interests. God is love, but He is also a consuming fire and disciplines us as children.

"For the Lord whom he loves disciplines and scourges everyone whom he receives as a son. If you endure discipline, God treats you as sons; for what son is he whom the Father does not discipline?" (Hebrews 12:6-7) He also says, "The Lord does not despise a grieved and humbled heart." (Psalm 51:17)

A true father loves his children and therefore instructs and disciplines them when there is a need. I humbled myself over and over again. Repented of all my transgressions and asked Him: "Lord, help me, I don't know what else to do from the bottom of my heart, forgive me and deliver me." And this time, my soul was broken and seeking in the spirit a fullness and affirmation in God. I reaffirmed my convictions in the Lord and decided, for the second time, to be baptized in the waters, now with more awareness, conviction and revelation. Now I was eager for the supernatural. I consecrated myself to the Lord, I renounced and turned away from conscious and unconscious iniquities, and I participated in retreats of liberation and inner healing. I learned to receive what Jesus has done for me, as the Spirit taught me, and to apply the Word, a process that took some time. At that stage of my life, I took the Bible more seriously, and in prayers, I learned to wage war in the spirit world. God and my leaders corrected me; they affirmed, ministered and delivered me, strengthening my life. In moments of weakness and sadness, Jesus was always there.

God's Instruments

I am very grateful to have had many committed and sincere people in God at different stages of my life who have prayed for me and helped me in various ways. Thank you, Lord, for your willing vessels! Bless them with so much more in every area of their life, wherever they are. You know who they are. Many people from different countries and cultures have blessed me so much.

As I said, for years I didn't have a job so that I could go to the different daily prayer groups in my church. I used to get up and go very early in the morning, and after that, I would wait for the next prayer group, also in the morning, with the pastor. I used to arrive home on many occasions around noon, since the early hours of the morning were spent in prayer in church. My day, despite everything, was joyful and full of peace. Also, in that same church, they had a 24-hour prayer every month. I used to spend long hours each month there, praying and pouring out my heart before God, and interceding for others. We prayed with fire and power.

I'm going to bless someone

I was very active in the services and all the activities of the church. I went to mid-week and Sunday services, daily prayers, intercession, and to the Bible Institute. I lived in the church, in other words. I was taking classes for almost three years. I am thankful to the Lord that I had the courage and intelligence to learn and was able to go deeper into God, and had perseverance when things got difficult in my studies. Those subjects were not easy, and the teachers and curriculum of the Bible Institute were tenacious and very strict in terms of teaching and participation. A few months into the church, after my release from prison and my re-baptism, I felt a desire to serve and entered evangelism and follow-up ministry. Follow-up ministry in that church was the beginning of discipleship, where we phone the new converts, help them, pray for them, encourage them to attend, teach them about baptism, and drive them to and from church. Sometimes we spent two or three hours driving them to and from church. When I didn't have a vehicle, I asked someone to go with me to look for the person, or I paid for a taxi. Later, when God gave me a car, I used to drive them home. In those two ministries, I served the Lord for 7 years.

I also helped and ministered outside of the church, as the Lord allowed me, such as going to jail, ministering in people's homes, on the streets, going to hospitals, and more. I was fully immersed with the Lord and serving Him as well, not for a month, not for a year, but for years, my dear readers! I needed it. I faced many difficulties, for example, sometimes I needed to ask for a ride to go to church, since I didn't have a car yet. I used to walk long distances to get to church or my Bible Institute classes, on hot or rainy nights. Sometimes I used to go to church with an extra blouse and my Sunday little shoes in my bag, because of the long walk. I would get sweaty and smelly, so I would go to the bathroom and wipe myself with a towel. Then, I would take my blouse and my little body powder out of the bag and get ready for the service. After that, I would go and enjoy the service. Not many people knew all that I was going through, unless they discerned it in the spirit. I learned to be humble to seek God because I loved Him and longed for Him, not only for what I needed or what I wanted from Him, but because I longed for what was the Truth, His satisfaction and joy. I learned to enjoy the supernatural. I developed hope and faith and stopped complaining and seeing myself as the poor me (the victim). It was a time of challenges, a time to grow and be liberated, especially from myself. I had the revelation that everything would change when I submitted and surrendered everything. Nothing worked in my life before because I had a problem with authority figures. Since my childhood, I have had a distorted image of my father. At this time, I was free to discern and understand it; it was different at this time. I had upright mentors and tutors. People who told me the truth in love, with the authority of God, and the truth set me free.

The Lord wants us to die to ourselves. It must be 100 percent God and not us. It hurts, the flesh doesn't want to submit, the mind makes you resist, and if you let him, the devil shakes you and affects your emotions. But there is victory if we get up and move forward through the Holy Spirit.

I learned, as Joshua said.

"Now fear the Lord and serve him with integrity and truth; remove from among you the gods whom your fathers served on the other side of the river and in Egypt; and serve the Lord. And if you think it is bad to serve him, choose today whom you serve." (Joshua 24:14-15)

I couldn't stand between two thoughts, with one foot in God and the other out. I had a great need within me to seek and serve the Lord with my whole being. Leaving everything was not what I wanted or felt like doing in my heart.

The Holy Spirit rebuked me again and again and did not let me be comfortable for long with any of my carnalities, praise God! It was as if His fire was consuming me internally. Nothing I tried or did carnally brought me satisfaction or peace; momentarily, it could give me "satisfaction", but then it left me spiritually dead and empty. I took quality time to pray. I learned to commune with the Holy Spirit in my daily life. I learned to live my faith regardless of how I felt or reasoned. I realized that when I obey, I always have God supporting me, even if I don't understand Him. God is faithful.

Obedience brings blessings.

The Bible tells us that obedience is better than sacrifice. God is interested in forming His character in us. If we are His, we will have to let ourselves be moulded, or we will become poor wretches bearing bad witness to others, and we will not be able to enjoy the abundant life that Christ came to give us, as I once was, As He said, "*I have come to give you life and life in abundance. (John 10:10)*

Not just life, but an abundant life. I still have a long way to go, but He who has begun the good work in us is faithful to perfect it until the day of Christ, in me and you, my dear reader. Do not lose heart. Honestly, I was tired of wallowing in shame, guilt, betrayals, deceit, loss, rejection, and so much more. So, it was time to give up; at the end of the day, I didn't have much to lose.

Prophetic Dream - High-Level Processes

The Bible mentions that Jesus went into the wilderness. He says that the Holy Spirit led Him in Luke 4:1: *"Jesus, filled with the Holy Spirit, was led by the Spirit into the wilderness."*

We see this as His powerful initiation into ministry. Also, before the cross and His death, He went to Gethsemane, a re-enactment of tribulation and agony. I remember that before my most incredible brokenness, I often had a dream that haunted me. It happened to me on different occasions, but it had the same meaning. My dreams mainly revolved inside water.

In one of my dreams, I was high up in a tree looking down at some clean water. Inside me, I knew I had to jump into the water, but I was afraid of the depths, and I would probably have to swim. I just kept holding onto the branches of the trees. In my last dream of this series, probably years apart from the others, I was under the tree, and I saw a storm of muddy, yellow waters approaching me. It was a flood, dragging turbulent and dirty waters. I immediately climbed the tree and grabbed a branch. That branch broke off, and then I kept swinging from branch to branch, trying to hold on, and each of them would break. I grabbed the last one from the tree, and to this day, I can hear the rustling of the branch breaking. The tree ran out of more branches, and I had no choice but to throw myself into the water. When I jumped, I was terrified of what would happen to me, but when I fell into the water, they were very clear. I didn't have to fight or even move my hands to swim or do anything because the river and its waters were bringing me afloat and I didn't have to stroke or exert any force. The waters carried me and were calm and clean. I floated on my back in the water, and the river took me. I felt at peace and even rejoiced to know that I didn't have to fight. I understood what God was saying to me. He was affirming and confirming to me the whole process that lay ahead of me before a deep brokenness occurred, and how I would overcome by surrendering to the Holy Spirit. Processes in God and with God are necessary if we understand them and collaborate with the Lord. Before all that, the word "process" sounded like something from hell to me, a terrible thing. But with time and God's revelation, I realized that many times we bring about the consequences, and other times God allows processes in our lives to form and build us from within. The Christian character and formation of Christ in us is like gold that is refined by fire.

Well, since that dream, storms of different challenging situations have come into my life. But if God is with us, who can be against us? He took me by the hand, wanted the best for me and helped me to this day.

I need more of Him every day. Each of us needs an encounter with the Holy Spirit. I was heartbroken, but this time, something perfect came out of it. I also understood what was happening and what to look forward to, because God was with me. I felt that God had allowed me to be naked and not be held up by any of the things I was trying so desperately to hold onto. I humbled myself and cried with all my heart. I had hit rock bottom and needed a transformation in my life. I had to learn to depend on Him and not on man or anything else. All those iniquities that I had opened doors to had to be eradicated from my life, and all those traumas and wounds had to be healed. But the Lord was there, I could feel His presence and His love near me. It hurts, but God disciplines us because we are sons and daughters, not bastards. I'm not saying that God goes around crushing people. God is a good Father, but in my case, He has had to deal very hard with my soul and human nature. The purpose of every child of God should be to give glory to Him and bring forth fruits that glorify His name and majesty.

That inner voice speaks to me

Even though I was going through the desert, filled with so many trials and processes, I continued to seek the Lord and be a blessing to others. I had that inner voice that encouraged me to keep going. I set out to serve others and build others up. I began to come out of myself. Serving others is one of the most beneficial things we can do when faced with various trials, challenges, struggles, and difficulties in our lives. In evangelism, I love sharing the good news of Jesus with others. I disciplined myself with the help of the Holy Spirit to spend time faithfully with the Lord, go to prayer groups, pray for others, for myself, and for my family.

Dear reader, it doesn't matter how many times you have to start again. Go back to basics, it's never too late, and it's never in vain. If we sincerely humble ourselves and believe in the one true God, we will succeed.

I was in my forties when I decided to let God be Lord in my life, when I desperately called from the depths of my heart once again to change me and give me a different life. The Lord delivered me from pride, hardness of heart, disobedience, idolatry, lying, religiosity, the spirit of independence, fear, malice, darkness, insecurity, avarice, and much more, as I have already told you.

I graduated in December 2013 from the Bible Institute. It was a great day for me to graduate from a Bible school; it was a great accomplishment and a great blessing. As I said, I was under the supervision of leaders and people assigned to help me within the church and within the institute, who helped me grow more in God. I had learned that my soul needs to prosper, and for this, we must grow in knowledge and revelation of the Word. We need to not only learn about the Word but also apply it in our lives.

Our soul and our mind do not want to give up; we like to think and do our way, and what we want and believe we should do. But the Bible exhorts us to renew our minds.

"And be not conformed to this world, but be transformed by the renewing of your mind, that you may prove what is the good, pleasing and perfect will of God." (Romans 12:1-3)

It also says that God wants us to prosper as our souls prosper. "Beloved, I desire that you be prosperous in all things and have health, just as your soul prospers." (3 John 2) For our souls to flourish, we must learn and follow God's Word. I needed to forgive and seek forgiveness from those I hurt. I had to release control and entrust my life to God.

At last, I let Him carry me on. Glory to His name forever! Hallelujah!

Chapter 13
Time on TV and Radio

The Lord began to open doors for me to preach, witness, and minister outside of my church. A dear sister who believed in what the Lord was doing in my life gave me, for about two years, a 3-minute capsule on her TV show to minister to women. The name of my friend's program was "The Word in Action." The name of the capsule was Para ti Mujer (for you women). Those minutes were glorious. In three minutes, I had to greet, establish a foundation of God's Word, minister to women, and close the section, sometimes encouraging or with an invitation to practice what I spoke to them, or to come unto Christ.

I made the television capsules with a grateful heart, a great love for God, and trusted that someone, through television, would be edified and blessed. I used to come out of that study filled with the Holy Spirit. Full of the joy of God. I also knew in my spirit that I was setting those words as breakthroughs in my own life—in the air and the heavens. Those words that came out through the airwaves were seeded and made their way. They established something powerful in the lives of other women, including my own and that of my loved ones. It felt so real. How glorious it is to serve the Lord! I borrowed clothes from my roommate or my sister, depending on where I was, to take advantage of this opportunity because I didn't have much to wear. Sometimes, I would leave the house to go to the TV station two to three hours in advance because I needed to take public transportation. I had to cross the entire city when I was living with my sister because I was travelling from one end of the town to the other, and it took hours by bus to get where I was going. The same sister in Christ of the TV's program, and I would also visit a local radio station, where God would use both of us.

Today, I say: Lord, you are faithful; thank you. I know that You are just God. You remember and do not forget what Your people have done for Your sake. I went through many needs, and God allowed me to be naked before Him, without a mask or covered by fig leaves. All my disobedience and stubbornness, for not letting Him disinfect my wounds, all of that had to go. Not as a punishment, but out of love. The Bible also states that it is a terrible thing to fall into the hands of the living God. Stubbornness is risky and leads to many negative consequences. When we have wounds and pain, the first and best thing we can do is seek the healing of those wounds, cleanse them, and receive God's medicine through His Word. Believe me, the Holy Spirit is there to help you and me.

Healing has already been provided for us on the Cross. It all begins with sincerely forgiving and completely yielding ourselves. Although I knew how to do good, I didn't do it; I walked my own way. The Bible says: He who knows how to do good and does not do it, sins against Him. (James 4:17)

Christ paid for us and gave us victory on the Cross, but our defective nature and mind must be renewed and healed. *"I beseech you, therefore, brothers and sisters, given the mercy of God, to offer your bodies as a living, holy, and pleasing sacrifice to God; this is your true rational worship. Do not conform to the customs of this world, but be transformed by the renewing of your mind. Then you will be able to test and approve what God's will is: His good, acceptable, and perfect will." (Romans 12:1-4) "We need to be doers of the Word, not just hearers." (James 1:22)*

Many of God's people talk and even minister about how Christ has done it all, and that we don't need to do anything else. It's true that He paid our sins, healed and delivered us on the cross, but we can lack the sincerity and honesty to recognize that we deal with things in our minds and our souls every single day. We need to let God, through His Holy Spirit, deal with us; we will always drag things with us, and we will not see the full manifestation of the Father. Without renewing ourselves and dying to our ways, we will not be much different from the rest of the world that does not know the Father through Jesus. All of us, at some point in our lives, must stand naked before God and look ourselves in the mirror (spiritually speaking). *"Behold, I will bring healing and medicine, and I will heal them." (Jeremiah 33:6) "But as for the past way of life, put off the old man, who his deceitful desires have corrupted." (Ephesians 4:22)*

Here is a question for you: Who strips off his old nature-flesh-desires? Does God strip you? Does anybody else strip you off? No, we must strip ourselves of the desires of our flesh. It is my responsibility to detach myself, to turn away, to renounce, and to resist as the Bible says: *"Submit therefore to God; resist the devil, and he will flee from you." (James 4:7)*

In my case at that time, I had lost everything except my breath after "having everything" materially. But afterwards, I found satisfaction and peace. We can have a house but not a home. We can buy medicines, but not health. We can buy a bed, but we can't buy the sleep. God showed me my inner self and my needs.

What we have inside we attract to ourselves. Rejection attracts rejection, a spirit of victimhood attracts insecurity, fear, control, manipulation, and religiosity.

My relationship with Jesus was and is everything I had in my life. I was in the middle of the world, with nothing and no one to turn to. What could be shaken was shaken, and what could be taken away was taken from my life. I had lost everything; only Jesus and His Word were my sustenance. He is the immovable Rock of the ages. I felt the pain of my disobedience, and even though I knew the Lord had forgiven me and was with me, there were moments of sadness for all that I had done and lost, and all I had caused myself and others.

Stubbornness costs us a lot. It almost cost me my life.

"He is the potter; we are the clay." (Isaiah 64:8)

He wants to form us, but we must let Him work. His Spirit is within us, but our character in Christ needs to be formed, our souls need to be healed and delivered, and our minds need to be renewed.

We are but clay, but He is the potter. We are the work of His hands. The Bible tells us,

"Everyone who calls on the name of the Lord must turn away from iniquity." (2 Timothy 2:19) Nevertheless, the solid foundation of God stands, having this seal: The Lord knows those who are His. Let everyone who mentions and calls on the name of the Lord turn away from iniquity.

I went through arid seasons of one process after another and great challenges in my life over 8 years. Those have been the hardest years of my life. Many times I felt alone, not listening to God at all, but, despite everything, I learned to let go, trust, and let God work for me, even though he had to deal with me in a significant way due to my nature and internal issues. I had nothing to lose but much to gain if I just yielded my life. I couldn't afford not to do the Father's will. That is how I gradually became intensely thirsty for more of God's presence. Now was not the time to look for culprits; I needed to give up and get up at any cost. The spiritual desert and Gethsemane are not comfortable places; it is not easy in our flesh, but it is a place of training and refinement of our souls. In the deserts, we learn to trust only in the Word and in the presence of God. And in Gethsemane, we learn to say, "Lord, let not my will, but Yours be done." Jesus Himself had to go to the wilderness and Gethsemane. I consider them places represented in our spiritual walk.

It was through several difficult years that God dealt with me until I was able to renounce my wrongdoing and began to submit my soul and mind to God wholly and willingly. He continues to this day to build me up. I am here because of his mercy and grace. I still have a long way to go because we have not yet reached perfection, as the apostle Paul said:

"But one thing I do: forgetting what is behind and striving for what is ahead, I press on toward the goal of the prize of God's upward calling in Christ Jesus." (Philippians 3:12-14)

Dear reader, if you are one of those who find yourself, whether in the desert or the place of Gethsemane, or any other place of anguish, struggles needs, or longing for more, I can tell you that, if you decide to seek Him and yield and give yourself to Him, with all of your heart, I am sure that you will see the glory and goodness of your Father.

I learned that our wrong choices, deliberate disobedience, and fleshly desires can lead to much pain and negative consequences. Satan tries to distract us from our purpose and steal our identity as children of God. In my case, my childhood and the poor decisions I have made were the biggest influences on me.

The Lord is good, very patient, and He gives us one opportunity after another. He loves us, teaches us, embraces us, gives us dreams and visions, and He sends people to teach us to help us. He has given us His Holy Spirit, all the weapons and provisions we need. The Holy Spirit reveals His Truth to us. Still, despite everything, if we continue in our stubbornness and insist on our ways, there comes a time when the Holy Spirit who led Jesus into the desert will also guide us to be stripped of our carnalities. I speak personally for myself and my experience. I know that God deals with each one differently.

But it is so powerful to know that: *"He who began a good work in us will complete it until the day of Christ." (Ephesians 1:6)*

Thanks be to the Lord who does not abandon us like bastards, but corrects us, moulds us, teaches us, and transforms us for his glory. I learned that if I want to walk with the Holy Spirit, I must be intimate with Him. I learned to commune with the Holy Spirit in my daily life, to have a relationship with my Father.

I slowly learned to live my faith despite how I felt. All those things at that time, I did not understand, spiritually and naturally. Our emotions should not direct us in our walk of faith. We need to walk by faith and not by sight. I have learned to depend on His Word through His Holy Spirit.

I learned that God is a righteous judge, and I need to close the doors to sin and conscientious disobedience. I realized that by obeying Him, I always have God's best for me, even if, for a while, I don't understand Him. God is faithful and is a covenant God. Above all, I needed to be willing and obedient.

Maybe you're reading this book, but you can't relate to any of my struggles, traumas, and life challenges. Perhaps you know someone who identifies with what I've gone through in my life. Please recommend this book to them. Hopefully, this book will open his/her eyes and touch them. My prayer and hope are that my story of God's mercy and grace will bring hope to others. I pray that they will identify with some area that I have dealt with, and that they will be encouraged and challenged to change or yield to the Lord completely.

I heard His voice and His promise.

All I wanted at that point was to be filled with His presence, to walk where He wanted me to walk, and to do what He wanted me to do. I was desperately hungry and thirsty for the truth and for my life to be changed radically. I made Psalms 103:1-5 my prayer. I used to say, *"Lord, I know there's more for me. I know that you are the ONE who forgives all my iniquities, the one who heals my diseases and brings my life out of the pit and destruction." (Psalm 103:1-5)* Fill me more with You and less of me. Father, use me for Your glory.

I lived only on God's Word and His presence; even though my outer world had collapsed, I continued to stand and believe, waiting on Him. Some of my loved ones used to make fun of me, directly or indirectly, sometimes with sarcasm. Some would hear me testify about the Lord and bear witness of my faith despite my natural conditions, saying words like, "Joselyn, I have heard you, that you're with Jesus, but look at you, where is He? I've listened to you for so long, and He still doesn't do anything for you. You have to be realistic and put your feet on the ground." I also heard: "I think you have become fanatical; you have to be careful." "Churches are only making money from people like you," and there were so many expressions of unbelief and ignorance. But I kept my face looking up, moving forward and seeking my Lord. I knew that I was not serving an impersonal God or religion, but that I was having a relationship with the Highest, a loving, powerful, and living God, the Creator of heaven and earth. The Truth of God needs to be revealed, and we are not called to argue but to love and to be a witness. I needed to continue to love my people, my family, and those around me, and pray for them.

Rolling all over without a place to live

I moved in with a friend. I ran from one place to another, wherever I could go, and people gave me a hand. My good friend Susana (the family therapist who talked about the book on the first pages) opened the doors of her small one-bedroom apartment. She is a beautiful soul and sister in Christ. At that time, she was a psychology student with many financial needs in her life, but she loved me and voluntarily gave me a hand. We used to have a good time praying and fasting together. She also lived with another faithful sister, my dear Ruth, also a student, so we were three in a tiny apartment, but we were all at peace, joyful and seeking the Lord with all our hearts and sharing the little we had with each other.

One morning, after spending some time with God, I began to write. The words came from within and from the center of my heart to my mind. The inner voice said, "A man will come from afar, he has a noble heart, he will accept you as you are, he will love you and help you." That was in 2010. It was something so real inside me that I cried. I wrote everything in my notebook and dated it. Hallelujah! I already perceived the voice of the Lord before all this, that I was not going to be alone for the rest of my life. I also knew inside me that the person I would meet and whom I would marry was not going to be from my land and culture. But I didn't know where he was going to come from, Hispanic, American, African, European, or who knows where. I only knew that he would come from afar, and now it was confirmed by the word given to my spirit on this specific day. I used to pray and thank the Father for His Word and remind the Lord of His promises. After receiving the word, I made a prophetic act of faith. Every day, I thanked the Lord and drew closer to God, letting Him deal with my soul.

I became fully involved in serving others, both in the church and elsewhere. It wasn't easy, but I no longer thought of the challenges and the process as a punishment from God, instead l saw it as something that was for my good, even though I did not understand it at the time, the Lord was allowing it to align my life and help me grow and be delivered from myself and the work of the enemy. I was also learning to close doors that gave legality to the enemy to steal from me or hinder what the Lord had already given me on the Cross.

Habitual sins open the doors for familiar spirits to infiltrate and try to wreak havoc, harm us, and take us back to the same sins we had in our lives and are familiar with. Sometimes, we repeat the same thing, and then we end up having an endless warfare in a situation or in an area where we choose not to obey. It is wise to examine ourselves and say,

"Show me your ways, Lord, make my way straight and give me revelation in the area where there is an open door that I must close. Give me wisdom to repent sincerely, and Your strength to obey You, Father."

An evil/sinful door closes by sincerely repenting, renouncing whatever we know is wrong, breaking the bond with it, and obeying God's word no matter what.

Here is an example of how to pray if you have doors open:

First, recognize your faults and shortcomings from the heart and with faith pray, "Father, forgive me for the sin or sins of... (mention it). I consciously and voluntarily decided to give it up. I detach myself in the name of Jesus and break all union with the spirit or attitude behind this disobedience in my life. Lord, You already made provision on the Cross. Cleanse this area with Your Blood and fill every void in my life with your Holy Spirit. I close every door that I have opened and given rise to evil legality in my life, in the Name of Jesus Christ."

Of course, this is just a model or example. You pray as the Lord leads you, and then yield, turn yourself around, and obey with joy. We can all do it. God has given us His Holy Spirit, His authority, the Blood, the Name above every name, and His Word. The choice is ours. God gives us the power and the will to make choices. The choice is yours.

My days as a teacher

As I grew closer to God and became freer every day, the Lord opened the doors for me to have a good job. I started working as a teacher, and I worked for several years. Being a teacher of children also helped me with healing in my soul.

God used my love for children and working with them to bring me more healing and joy to my soul. By being a teacher of young children, and by being close to them, helping and loving them, I was healing a part of myself, of my childhood, and the lack of being with my children that I was missing. I remember those days very gratefully. God allowed me to work as a teacher for many years. I loved it. There are great memories and learning experiences. Children are such great teachers. God used the children, my students and some of their family members in a big way. This brought more healing and sensitivity to my heart.

Chapter 14
The Promise with Ugly Wrapping

After receiving the Lord's prophetic Word in late 2011, I met a man. We got to know each other excitingly and uniquely. (That's probably material for another book, God willing.) He was born again, and we were both attracted to each other. He travelled to Santo Domingo to meet me personally. He came through the Punta Cana airport and took a bus to the capital, where I lived, 4 hours away. I had a lot of questions at first. Christ was the center of my life. I wanted to serve and please Him, despite everything. I was actively involved in the service of Jesus, and I was aware that my relationship with God, if I were not intentionally focused, could grow cold or be affected by a wrong decision or relationship in my life. I was already very aware of my choices at that time. My biggest concern when I met a man interested in me was that we could fall into sexual relations or that he didn't want to wait, and I would give in. I wanted to please the Lord from the bottom of my heart. My suitor and I shared time. He met part of my family, some friends and visited my work. We talked a lot and went out to eat and see places. We talked about different things, family, dreams, God, church, and he told me he was single. We connected. He expressed his interest in me and seemed happy and confident in what he was doing and what he wanted. We shared a week in my country, then he returned to Canada. We stayed connected, on the phone and writing to each other, until the man, for no reason, disappeared after a few weeks, no calls, no texts, no emails.

Wow. I wondered, "What happened here? What was going on?" I was very confused. I was trying to understand the puzzle. But even with this emotional and spiritual shock, I chose to continue to humble myself before the Lord. I still wondered what was going on; it was painful, I can't deny it. I thought I'd been kidded or something. I continued to write to him and asked him what had happened and why he hadn't written to me. I asked him what was wrong with him. I told him, "I thought you were sincere." At my insistence, I wrote to him again, expressing my confusion and desire to know the truth, and asking him why he had disappeared. The reality is that I had believed everything he had told me. Why did he make promises and then disappear? I wondered. I began to think that this man was sick, that he had serious problems, he was a maniac or something like that. Well, he finally replied to one of my emails explaining what happened.

The man wrote to me and told me that he had returned to someone he had been involved with for several years. According to him, they were separated and, at the time, were just friends. He said he was sincere in everything he had told me. He explained that his ex-partner returned and knew that he had come to my country to meet me. She ran to look for him and insisted on restarting her relationship with him, and he decided to accept her back again. More pain was added to my life. Why did he lie or not tell the truth about his life? I kept asking myself.

Through it all, with confusion and frustration, I didn't stop from continuing to draw closer to God, look to Him, and seek Him even more deeply. I was learning to draw near to God instead of running away from Him, as I used to, even in the face of ugly and painful challenges. I kept humbling myself before the Father, and I kept crying out to Him, taking special time for Him. The only thing that was true to me was my Heavenly Father, and I've learned not to rebel or run away from Him. That was a test that I finally passed. Before, I used to rebel against God and get depressed or hide and get under a shell like a turtle. I was determined not to run away from Him anymore or return to my old weaknesses. I was learning to persevere, to be of one mind, and to know who I am in Him, and through Him, my identity was developed.

Jesus was and is my focus. Everything else is secondary. I came to a position where I said that if I live or die, it is with Him. In my case, God had to allow the breaking of my life so that I would be free and heal all those wounds and extract the pus and the infections from them. The healing of our souls hurts, as well as our spiritual growth. See how I emphasized healing in our souls, because in our spirits, we are complete when we receive Christ.

God's Character

Well, back to my suitor. As I mentioned, he finally admitted that he had given his ex-partner one more chance. That was devastating for me. Although he liked me, he admitted that he was also afraid and concerned due to our distance, different cultures, and customs, among other things.

This left another wound in my heart, but at that moment, the urgency of the Holy Spirit was digging deeper into me, and my only refuge was Christ. I refused, through it all, to go back to my old ways. My character was growing strongly within me. Christ was supporting me; and I kept humbling myself and serving as He guided me.

The Lord Jesus and my service to Him in the church as an evangelist, going out to the streets, hospitals, and homes, was very satisfying, and the Follow-Up Ministry was my engine to move forward.

I faithfully went to prayer meetings with fire prayer warriors filled with the Holy Spirit. I prayed and fasted like you wouldn't believe. I learned to treasure the presence of God. I can sincerely tell you that I have many memories and experiences of those years. It is imperative to seek and serve the Lord, not as a ritual or a religious spirit, but in spirit and truth in a deep relationship with Him. God did not send Jesus to create a religion, but He longs to have a relationship with us as a Father to His sons and daughters.

I am thankful for so many of God's people in my life. I always pray for those who have blessed my life in different seasons. May the Lord give them twice as much for their service of love, patience, prayers, and impartation in my life and the lives of so many others.

I wanted a different life. When we are of God, He leads us to the death of self. At that time, even when I was going through the biggest spiritual process of my life, I got involved in helping others, and I also enrolled in my local church's Bible Institute because I wanted to learn and be able to serve God effectively. It hasn't been easy; none of us has been on top of the mountain all the time. I sought Jesus with the longing for His healing to be manifested in my life and to leave behind all the bonds and structures within me. The Lord has given me strength, kept me, and encouraged me continually. Inside, despite myself, there was always that burning fire that wouldn't let me go until I did what He said. All glory to Him ! I had to learn a lot, and now that I was open and honest with myself, I became teachable and accepted corrections. In other words, I humbled myself and let go of pride. I suffered in my flesh. The flesh does not want to submit, nor to surrender, but I was ashamed of my ways, and I asked for forgiveness. I learned to fight against the spirit of condemnation and guilt that the enemy of the soul uses to keep us with our heads down. None of those spirits is from the Lord. He is a God of love and freedom. I cried out to God and sought the Lord with all my heart against all odds, and He was there with me. For some things, I didn't see immediate answers; those years were like a season of believing and growing without any encouragement from heaven, without hearing or seeing. Just believing and persevering. I went through many years in the desert, and all I had were His Words, His promises, and faith that His presence was with me.

I needed to be restored and healed in my soul, and I needed my mind to be renewed.

I believe that a powerful weapon of victory is perseverance. Perseverance is a weapon of war, persevering in prayer, in the Word, continuing to trust and look up when everything is dark and there is not much light ahead. Struggles and challenges bring out the diamond within us when we walk through them with the Lord. If we are to be established and fruitful in the Kingdom of God, we must go through shaking, brokenness, and refinement to fulfill our God-appointed purpose. God uses cracked and broken vessels. God deals with our will. We need to surrender our will. The refinement, the polishing, is when we come to the point: "Lord, what do you want to do with me? O Lord, what do you want me to do?" Olive oil comes from the crushing of olives. It produces a good oil. All those years of hardship produced in me a holy character and an inner strength of iron and convictions that I would need for the rest of my life.

Stripped of everything

My identity was beginning to be defined, and Christ's authority in me was developing. Today, I have been able to remain in the Lord for those years of being stripped of everything that I thought was valuable in life, all my dependence on people and things. At that point in my life, there was only one alternative: I would surrender completely to Christ, or I would keep tripping over the same stone and maybe even lose my life prematurely along the way. I chose to surrender and let the Lord shape me. Or I should say, "He brought me to the point of giving up." Some days weren't easy; sometimes, I wanted to jump off the boat, but something inside me gave me hope and encouragement despite how things looked and felt outside. That's the Holy Spirit. There were times when I didn't have much to drink or eat, not even clothes to wear. I had nowhere to go, no money, no job, not even a few close people to turn to. The isolation and loneliness were real, but this was necessary to deal with my soul; God always supplied and opened a path out of nothing.

I passed the test. The man came back

In late 2012, almost a year after my suitor met me, I was on my computer and saw a message arriving in my email from Donald Jenkins. I was in shock; I couldn't believe it for a moment. Was he the same Donald Jenkins I knew? I wondered. I opened the email, read it, and there was Donald, whom I had met about a year prior, asking me to forgive him for the pain he had caused me and for the way he had made me feel. He asked me if we could be friends again.

He was back to being single and not engaged to anyone. I was committed to the Lord and didn't want any relationship that didn't come from my Father. All I wanted to do was God's will and do things God's way. I didn't want to get involved anymore with someone who wasn't sure it was God's will for me, and I was so busy with the Lord and serving others that I didn't have much time to think about getting a man. I was entirely in love with Christ. I came from a church that had about 4,000 or more members at that time, and I hadn't dated anyone in the church. I had no problem telling him that I forgave him and that we could communicate again as friends. We started talking and calling each other. He told me how he decided to leave his ex-partner because he needed a woman who loved God. He had seen my consecration and love for the Lord. We began to get to know each other more deeply as friends.

Donald made another trip to the Dominican Republic to get to know me and my family deeply. Truth be told, my pastors, in their love and concern, were not very happy that I was dating a man in a long-distance relationship, but I prayed, asking the Lord for His direction and wisdom and confirmation if it was His will.

Donald came back to my country a couple of times, and we talked about everything. He was honest and showed a lot of interest; he didn't disappear anymore. I asked the Lord to confirm for me. I said, "God, I am going to tell this man all my life, if this relationship is Your will, he will accept me, and I will not talk about it anymore. If it is not Your will, he will be gone forever." Well, the day came when I told him everything about my life, with all the details, but his response was, "That was your past, I am a man forgiven by God, too, and I need Him more than ever." I was happy to hear that, because I came from relationships where I trusted my partners and told them about my life, or at least parts of it. That same truth would come back to me and be thrown in my face every time I argued, or we had disagreements. In the past, my son Jesse's father didn't forget anything I told him. He called me all kinds of names and humiliated me with everything he knew about me, from past relationships. I tried to be honest and open, but that cost me dearly later. I was humiliated by the very things I confided in him. So that was a good answer, according to what I had asked the Lord. We dated each other for a few months, connected through calls, emails, and text messages. I made sure to communicate with people who knew him personally and could provide information about him. I continued to pray and fast.

I received words that confirmed what I was asking the Lord, and I understood. We were getting more personal. He said he was also praying that I would give him a new opportunity to start over. One day, I told him very clearly, "Donald, I know what I want in my life. Do you know what you want for sure? Because I'm not here to waste time at my age. I want a union where Christ is the center, and I want my partner and I to live for Him and serve Him." He replied: "I, too, have suffered a lot in life, and I want a true Christian home. I have had other relationships with women who claimed to be Christian, but in the end, the result has not been the best." I replied, "Now, with my relationship with Christ, I am very serious;

I'm not playing. For me, it's God's way or nothing. We need to pray and seek guidance on what is the best decision for us." Donald talked to his children about me and told them he wanted to get married, and they agreed. I also received signs and confirmation from God.

God gave him a sign

According to what Donald told me, it was God who gave him my email one night when he was sleeping. He said he had deleted all my information previously when he was with his ex-partner again. When they finally separated, he regretted getting back to her, because he felt that he had hurt me. Some time after, he realized that he had made a big mistake by going back to his previous relationship. He was constrained and very sad. He had a vision in which he saw my email on the wall, suddenly woke up, and wrote it down on a piece of paper. He then wrote back to me. He sincerely believed that this was a sign to him. I am relating what he said.

God is good. He affirms things to us before we begin the process so that we have an anchor of His covenant and guidance for us. I prayed for a different kind of love relationship, a godly relationship in which Jesus would be welcomed with His Power and purpose for us. Because of my relationship history, at the beginning, I was a little reflective. I didn't want anything or anyone to hinder my relationship with the Lord. My past had cost me a lot, so I had to be careful. I didn't want to get involved with the wrong person again, but I felt at peace with the decision to get married. We took the time to pray. So, we agreed to get married. With the decision came more peace in my heart, and a new joy; I was excited.

We began preparations for the wedding. We didn't want anything luxurious, but a celebration with some family and friends. We didn't have a lot of money for the celebration, so unfortunately, we couldn't invite all the members of the family. I have a large family. My God, those days were glorious! Smile. After the decision to get married, we were already walking toward the destination, constantly praying and preparing.

For me, it was like a fairy tale. I was close to being fifty years old, and I could be reborn to love again in my heart. The joy of having someone who values, loves, respects and admires me was very satisfying. I barely slept during those days of preparation. I was like Dad's little girl, whom He had forgiven, purified, and moulded, preparing me for the big wedding event. I decided to have someone make my wedding dress by hand. The seamstress said, "Joselyn, do you prefer a cream colour? Because you've been married before and because of your age." To which I replied, "I want my dress to be the colour I am feeling inside, and I see my soul right now as white, and an accentuated white.

So my dress and the ornament on my head were very white. Praise God.

There will be no sex until marriage.

A few months before the wedding, Donald helped me rent an apartment with furniture. I moved from my previous home, which was a room in my dear friend Gloria's house. To the new apartment that would be our matrimonial home until the day I could go to be with my husband in Canada, or so we thought. It was a small, furnished apartment in a good area of the capital, with air conditioning, a small terrace in front, and everything we needed. From the beginning of our relationship, I set the boundary that there would be no sex until marriage, and he agreed.

I had learned to keep myself consecrated for the Lord. I was serving and actively participating in my place of worship, and my spiritual muscles were strengthening. Therefore, I already had a great awareness of my accountability and respect for God, a reverent fear. I knew by revelation that holiness and righteousness are beneficial to his house (us). God is a Holy God. He said: Be holy, for I am Holy.

Being obedient was and is today so much better than a moment of pleasure for me. Having to start over or lose everything I had, it had already happened to me so many times. But at that moment, the reverent fear of God was within me. Look at how I emphasize "reverent awe"; a fear of respect, of submission to a good Father who knows what is best for me and who wants my good and has plans for good and not evil. Although God forgives us when we come to Him truly repentant, there are consequences for our actions contrary to the Lord's will.

I needed to give up those areas every single day to see the Lord's faithfulness and prosperity manifest in my life. Therefore, it was, and still is, crucial for me to be in tune with my Father's will and to walk uprightly, to commune with Him, to seek His face, not out of religiosity, self-righteousness, or pride, but out of love for Him. Everything we receive is not because of who we are or what we do, but it is because of His grace. The Kingdom of God has laws to which its citizens must submit.

It was worth it for me to consecrate myself

I could do whatever I wanted at that time. I was a single woman, an adult, finally free from all the violence and oppression of the past, but I had to give an account to God, who sees and knows everything. I was set apart and consecrated for Him. That sounds to somebody like: Oh, that's a holy religious saint! I'm not talking about being perfect, but about having a mind and a feeling for God and His reality in our lives and wanting to grow and be transformed. It is possible through His Holy Spirit and a burning desire to be what He wants us to be, even though we all have a long way to go. I recognize that I am far from being perfect; no one is perfect, only God. I want to grow in dependence on the Lord and enjoy my days. There is fear of punishment, which is not the fear we should have of God. There is also a fear that comes from respect and reverence that is manifested by respecting and worshiping our Heavenly Father out of love and gratitude.

The Bible says, *"The fear of God is the beginning of wisdom." (Proverbs 9:10).* I learned and I am still learning to fear Him with reverence and respect, not as I used to fear my earthly father with dread. God, as a true and good Father, deserves our love, respect and trust.

Chapter 15
The big day, my marriage

Donald arrived a day before the wedding. The next day, July 5, 2013, was my big day. I left early for the hairdresser's salon. I remember the line of women waiting at the hairdresser's was extraordinary (women filled beauty salons on weekends). I spent so much time at the hairdresser's that part of my family thought I had gotten lost, or maybe I had been kidnapped. It seems funny, but it's true. Finally, I arrived at my sister's house. I got dressed there, surrounded by my mother, my sister, and her children. They helped me put on that beautiful dress made just for me. After getting dressed and putting on makeup, everything moved very quickly. We went to the place where the wedding and the celebration would take place. My husband met me at the ceremony, and we celebrated at the appointed time. Some of my close relatives attended. My mother, some of my brothers and sisters, my son Aneurys, his wife and son Gabriel, my son Jesse, some close friends, my boss and her family, a musician, two photographers, the judge and the waiters were all waiting for me. I have a large family, but sadly, I couldn't invite them all because of the monetary budget.

I arrived at the place, a nice Middle Eastern-style restaurant with a beautiful activity room. My fiancé was eagerly waiting. He looked very well dressed, handsome and nervous. My son Aneurys was the best man. He waited for me outside with the pages, my nephew Ronald, my niece Kiara, and my grandson Gabriel. Aneurys took me by the hand to the sound of the music, and we entered the room. What a blessing to see my son proudly holding his mother by the hand, and I felt joyful that he gave me up. My two sons were present. Jesse came from Miami to be with me as well.

Everyone was standing, waiting to see the bride parade down the aisle to the sound of a beautiful song. The tables were extraordinarily well arranged with gold and white trim, and the restaurant displayed splendid decorations; it was a charming place. The waiters were very well dressed, standing waiting for the right moment to serve the people. The cameramen and some very well-dressed friends were on both sides, all looking at me and smiling as I passed through the corridor to go where the judge was waiting. I was joyful, nervous, and in tears. My family were amazed seeing this happening to me. A pastor friend of mine, his wife, and their two daughters were there, thrilled to see me happy. As always, my life was surrounded by children. My grandson Gabriel and my nephew Ronald were there with the rings. My niece Kiara was in the front with a basket of rose petals. We reached the end of the hallway. The judge stood near the small, beautifully arranged table and two chairs assigned to the bride and groom, which the restaurant had prepared for us to sit and celebrate the civil ceremony. My fiancé and I looked like young kids getting married for the first time. Smile. What the Lord does is incredible to human minds. He restored my purity and made all things new, glory to His name.

The ceremony took place, and I thanked all those present, first to the Lord Jesus Christ for allowing me to marry as a young virgin, with a very different man in my life. He is someone who values me and shows respect, love, and concern for me. I was so pretty in my snow-white dress, grateful and full of joy. It was a fairy tale to me. I thanked the people who were present and those who were not, but who were also part of me. I received congratulations and beautiful words from the audience for my husband and me. They gave us many gifts.

My two children were present, and I started crying deeply. As always, I usually cry for everything, but this time, I had tears of joy, gratitude, and a mixture of good emotions. Thank you, Father, I kept repeating it in my mind. We shared with those present. We ate, danced, and kissed. It was an unforgettable day for me; unlike anything I had experienced before. We all celebrated with joy, and then, my husband and I left for the honeymoon.

God changed my story. Praise His Holy name forever!

My Heavenly Father began to reveal His goodness and His glory openly in my life before everyone. The Lord replaced my dishonour with honour. Holy Father, how can I not adore and love you? How can I not be grateful?

Our honeymoon

We went to a resort for a few days after our wedding. I felt like a queen; my husband was different from all the men I had met before. I was so grateful and full of joy. I knew that I had met someone not perfect, but who would walk with me. We had so much fun at that beautiful resort and stayed close to the beach. In the Dominican Republic, there are many beautiful resorts and hotels. After the honeymoon days were over, we returned to the city and everyday life.

I continued in my regular job as an ESL teacher in a Montessori school. I also continued to serve God with all my heart and passion actively. My husband returned to his country, Canada, to work. We planned and had many dreams and desires to be together. We still did not know how our future would turn out, knowing my past mistakes and background, but we decided to depend on God and believe in Him. We had to present papers and fight to be together. Before we decided to get married, my husband and I consulted with a lawyer in Canada. Donald asked if I could travel there with a criminal record. The lawyer assured him that I could because the deportation was 10 years ago, and I was well behaved in my country, and a productive citizen who had never been involved in any other criminal activity. By that time, it had been more than 20 years since the sentence was handed down in my original case. My husband had to go back to Canada, so we separated at the airport, sad and tearful, but hopeful. We decided to believe and have faith. We prayed together and said goodbye. Now, I would adjust to being a wife and, at the same time, live without my partner for a while. My husband came to visit me every 3 or 4 months. We wanted to apply for residency so that I could go with him to Canada. We didn't have much knowledge of what to do, but we took a chance and started our application on our own. I looked up the application process on the internet, and we began the process of applying for it, without anyone's help.

Marriage in the Church

In my church, they have a general wedding every year to this day. Many couples marry at the same time or renew their vows before God. Don and I obtained our second renewal and commitment before the Lord in December 2013, six months after the civil marriage. My pastors married us before the Lord. It was a great blessing. It was a beautiful congregational wedding ceremony. Married couples need to commit themselves to the Lord, no matter how many times they do it. Marriage is a covenant, not a contract; we need to be reminded of it.

Deeper processes and challenges

After the honeymoon, we decided to apply for my residency, and we did our best without professional help. My husband travelled back to Canada, and we were hopeful that we would soon be together. Almost a year has passed since we applied, and finally, Immigration sent me the appointment for an interview. I was very nervous. My husband travelled to be with me for that interview.

The day came, and we went to the immigration office. I entered the interview room; they forbade my husband from entering. My interviewer was waiting for me. I looked at that tall man of colour; he had in his hands my FBI report, which I was required to submit with the application, because I had lived in another country. That report was inside my folders.

There was nothing wrong with the report; I had already served all my prison time. It only showed the history of my charges, the information about the court and time served, and all the records.

Upon entering the office, they asked me to sit down. The man with an intimidating face implied, "I am waiting to catch you." That was how I perceived it. He was in front of me and began the interview. I was shaking and unsure of what to expect. My heart was pounding, my hands were cold, and I could hardly speak. The interview started.

Here are some of the main questions from the interviewer: "How did you meet?" I explained to him how and when we met. He didn't consider how long we had known each other, shared, and communicated, but he counted the time we had spent together in real life.

The interviewer asked, "With so little time being together, how do you know this relationship will work?" I said, "It will work, we love each other." He asked me questions about my past, about my husband's past, and many other things.

The interviewer: "Who can assure you that you can go to Canada?" I assumed that he was probably speaking because of my criminal record; I humbly replied, "I am a Christian, my life is a new life, and I know that with God, nothing is impossible; this marriage is real."

The interviewer babbled some words that I didn't manage to hear, and with a face of 'I don't believe a single word of what you're telling me' (he didn't say that, but he implied it, judging by his facial expression and body language). He closed the interview, sealed a piece of paper that was on the table, and denied my request to go to Canada. That was a hard blow. I immediately began to think about Donald, who was outside. I wondered if he would be willing to endure and move forward, not knowing what to expect from that moment on. I left crying and stunned with so many emotions.

Outside that office, my husband was waiting. I went up to him and told him what had happened, sobbing, and he said, "Let's go on, Joselyn; I don't give up easily." I was happy to hear that, but it was a challenging and sad moment. I had many beautiful dreams of being with him and having a home to serve God together. We were knocked down, but inside, I felt that there was hope. I think Don felt the same way. I cried a lot, and that same night, these words came to me, as if echoing in my mind in the middle of the night while I was in bed, next to my husband.

"Thus saith the LORD: Refrain thy voice from weeping and thine eyes from tears, for thy labour shall be rewarded, saith the LORD."

I remember this word is in Jeremiah 31:16.

And "Why are you weeping now with a loud voice? Have you no King? Has your King perished? Is that pain like that of a woman in labour?" This word (Micah 4:9) also came to my heart and mind.

In my sobs, the uncertainty of the moment, and all the emotions, God, in His immense mercy and love for me, gave me His Word. I felt like He was correcting me. Don't you have a King? Why have you had birth pains as if you were an orphan? Did your counsellor die? I felt my Father's gentle correction, but also His encouragement. Hallelujah! Sometimes, when we are going through a valley or a desert, we forget the promises of the Lord, but He is there to uplift us.

The Lord is so good; there I was, being rebuked for my discouragement and unbelief, and I was also encouraged by His Word - Glory to God. What a good Father! A blow in the fight does not determine the war. We will rise again. We can be knocked out, but we are not defeated. When we believe, we get back up again and keep fighting and persevering.

Don returned to Canada after the interview, and I recovered with the strength that only the Holy Spirit could give. I had to keep going, persevering, and trusting in the Lord. A new supernatural force came into my life. Then, I had to make arrangements to move out of my place. We needed to save money for all the expenses associated with a new application, such as stamps, translations, certifications, legalization, medical checkups, application fees, reapplying for the FBI international background check, local background checks, and more. Now, we had to find a professional who could do things better, like a lawyer who would cost us a good amount of money. Immigration lawyers are not cheap. I moved to a more affordable place. I rented a room, living in the house of a sister in Christ from my church. Moving into her home was a great blessing, despite our differences. That sister's faith was strengthened, and we were able to help each other in the ways of the Lord. She allowed Donald to visit me. Even though I rented out one of her rooms in her house, I had the right to use the rest of the house, except for her room, of course.

The Lord helped, strengthened, and encouraged us.

A Powerful Vision of the Lord

In that house, I had a dream from the Lord regarding what was happening.

This was the dream:

I saw many people watching me from afar. I didn't know who they were, but I kept watching them. They were very tall. I couldn't tell if they were for me or against me. I looked at these tall people for a while, then started to worry and became concerned. They were observing me. Suddenly, I saw an apostle, not the apostle of my church, but his spiritual father interceding, making spiritual war, fighting in the spirit, praying for me, and defending me. Then I suddenly saw myself leaving the domain of the high people, but in a very unusual way. I was dressed in white, very white, like a bride. I was sitting in a river of calm waters, but the seas were pushing me out, and then

I woke up from my dream.

I fell asleep and had the same dream again, the same night, the second time. I woke up and asked the Lord, "What is this?" From then on, dear reader, hell and giants had been unleashed against me as if there was no tomorrow. More harsh challenges would occur.

We applied for my residency again, and my husband looked for a lawyer in Canada. During my second immigration application process, I discerned and discovered that there were investigators, police, immigration agents, and different government departments involved in my case, both from my country and internationally. Something beyond routine investigation was happening. spiritually, there were also human entities and evil spirits at work, trying to block my freedom and blessings. God showed me in the dream the giants; some of them were not against me, but others would use enemy tactics against me. Yet, He also revealed how my situation would end in victory, by pulling me out into those waters, dressed as a beautiful bride in white.

Investigators and strange people followed me to my church and work to ask about me, watching my every move. Others tried to discredit me, trying to make me fall into traps and hooks. I will call it that.

God showed me and granted me discernment. The Lord was giving me understanding and wisdom about what I should or shouldn't do. My phone was tapped. Many times, those responsible for justice in various countries abuse their power. I felt like I was under constant surveillance. I sensed spiritual attack from people the devil could use. I had no private life. My mind was alert and aware, and the Lord protected and shielded me. Sometimes I discerned, felt, and smelled spirits in my room.

Don't take me wrong, I understand the authorities, they need to do their job, and I have no problem with that, because I have nothing to hide or to be afraid of, by the grace of the Lord. But it is one thing to do the job and another to abuse positions and power.

Thanks be to the Lord, the most significant and most potent power of all is our Lord Jesus Christ. The system of this world does not believe in new life, repentance, and salvation, much less in those of us who are Christians, after being delivered from a dark past, but radical changes and transformations are possible with God's help, and I am a living testimony of that. Not everyone who goes to prison has a criminal mind.

God's Word says: "The Kingdom of God becomes strong, and only the mighty take it by force." (Matthew 11:11)

For those of us who are genuinely born again and are agents of light, darkness wants to inject fear and make others doubt us. We can doubt our identity if we are not careful or if we do not know who we are in Christ and the reality of the Kingdom of God. Therefore, if we say we are His, we must let His Spirit form the character and worth of Christ in us, and He strengthens us. Thank the Lord, at that time when I was in church, I was taught to face my weaknesses and sins and be vulnerable, and to strip naked without religiosity before the Father. In other words, I needed to be completely honest with myself, with God and with others. To look at myself in the mirror of the Word of God. I learned that when I received Christ, my spirit is connected to the Father, but my soul needs to surrender, and my mind needs to be renewed, day by day.

For many years, I was a Christian, but I didn't make much progress, because I let myself be carried away by natural, physical, and emotional needs or by what others said. Until I learned that my soul had to completely forgive, surrender, and yield to the Holy Spirit. In other words, subduing my flesh was spiritual gain.

The Word says, *"Jesus learned to obey because of what He suffered."*

Hebrews 5:8-10 says: "And though He was a Son, He [Jesus] learned obedience by the things He suffered; and having been perfected, He became the author of eternal salvation to all who obey Him; and He was declared by God to be a high priest after the order of Melchizedek."

And if that was Jesus, then he needed to obey. Imagine, my dear reader, what excuse do we have to refuse to learn and follow? Many of us have to go through some processes to learn to surrender our flesh, subdue our souls, let go, and thus obey. This was my case. There were many moments of anguish and uncertainty, but one thing was sure: I remained grateful to the Holy Spirit and under the protection of the Most High. Donald and I had challenging times, and when we felt like we couldn't take it anymore, the Lord strengthened and comforted us. I concentrated on obtaining all the necessary papers and having them professionally translated and certified. We kept trusting the Lord. There was one problem after another. Sometimes, we were required to resubmit the duplicate national and international police records after six months, because they are no longer valid after a few months. I once remember having to pay for a website to search for "international researchers", because they asked me to give an account of all the addresses, jobs, and activities I had done since I was 18 years old. Imagine, my dear reader, how I could remember all the addresses and details of my history at my age.

All immigration departments and agencies in the Dominican Republic were doing their job, but Father God, what an agonizing and tedious process that was. At that time, many things were going through my mind, but when I knelt and sought the Lord, He calmed me down and gave me peace and strength to my soul and mind to continue. My husband was also going through a rough time, for almost five years of struggles working and waiting for my residency. He travelled 15 times to my country, every 3 or 4 months. I am grateful for Don's sacrifices, even made with physical pain, as he needed knee replacements back then. He was travelling in excruciating pain and discomfort. Sometimes, after long hours of flight and a few stops, he would arrive in the DR almost crippled with pain. At the end of the day, since we got married, we waited nearly five years to be together as husband and wife in Canada.

My Case of Rehabilitation was approved

By the grace and power of my Father Almighty, I never stopped holding fast to His Word, promises, and covenant with us. As a song says: "Through it all, I learned to trust in Jesus, I learned to trust in God. Through it all, I learned to depend on His Word." In English, the title is "Through it all." That is my testimony in two lines. Finally, after so much waiting, through enduring so many wars, spiritual, mental, emotional, physical, and economic, immigration gave me an appointment for another interview. Donald was with me. We were informed that my case to prove that I was rehabilitated, which I submitted as part of my application for Canadian residence, was approved as genuine.

First, we needed to prove that our marriage was real. Now, I needed to prove that I was rehabilitated from my past and that I am who I told them I am, through another legal process.

I bet they already knew everything about me, but due to my criminal record, it was required. I would have to open another case and prove that I had rehabilitated myself from my past. Oh, Father, so many challenges.

When my lawyer found out, she asked for more money that we didn't have. My husband was exhausted from the long battles. But I regained my strength and talked to Don and said, "I'll do it with God's help. He will guide me on what we need and how to do it, without having to pay for a lawyer." We informed the lawyer, and she was not very happy, but she would still be my lawyer because the case was the same. I would keep her informed of my actions and send her everything. I was going to do what I could on my own.

God gave me the wisdom I needed

I had to find out on the internet how to apply and fill out the rehabilitation forms and start my case. I started filling out the forms, looking for all the people who knew me and could give references about me, who were willing to make affidavits about me and my life, and how I had lived and behaved in their midst. These documents involved members of my church, community, friends, work, family, and professionals, work letters, certification of good conduct, and an account of my life since I was 18. It outlined where I had lived and worked, and what I had done, detail by detail, without missing any interval of time. Thank God that after being incarcerated, I never had any criminal cases or anything to do with courts. I never even got a fine for driving in my country. After I finished the whole process of filling out the application and forms, by faith, I went to church and presented those papers at the Altar of God, and we prayed over them. I asked the warriors and prayer intercessors, and they supported me with prayer times.

Thank God for His people who pray and are sincerely involved with others. I did not lose heart in prayer, fasting, and praising the Lord. I also did not faint in what I was doing for God, as I was already aware that He was teaching me through my circumstances.

Throughout that process, I also learn why God sometimes denies or delays our requests. He is working on specific areas in our lives, such as pride, self-reliance, patience, perseverance, inner healing, and sins. Maybe He has something better for us, or He wants to mature us even more so that we can grow and give glory to Him alone. Or perhaps it is not the right time yet, because you are dealing with aspects of your purpose that need to be aligned for others, and they are not ready. But it is worth waiting and persevering in faith.

God is sovereign, and we know His Word. We cling to it in faith. We believe in Him, we seek Him, we long for Him, we persevere. But in the end, God also knows what is best according to His purpose for us and knows how to process us internally. God is faithful to His Word, but the manifestation of His response and timing belongs to Him alone. Many times, we delay the response with our attitudes, lack of obedience, faith, or integrity.

Some things that I had learned

We must pray without ceasing. The Word tells us, *"Pray without ceasing."*

(1 Thessalonians 5:17)

But we must also do our part on this earth. We cannot leave everything to God unless the Lord says to stay still. We must move forward, as God said to Moses, *"Take the rod and divide the sea." (Exodus 14:14)*

We should make decisions with the help of the Holy Spirit and keep going.

Faith without works is dead.

As I wait, I must persevere, praise, and thank God. To rejoice in the God of my Salvation and to be satisfied with Him. It's good and wise to bless someone else while your answer is on the way. Serve another, help, and pray for others. It is essential to keep our eyes, heart, and hope on Jesus Christ, not on humans, in myself, the system, or the government.

"Fixing our eyes on Jesus, the author and finisher of faith."

(Hebrews 12:2)

Sometimes we should pray and then wait for God to take the steps that only He can take. When we obey and persevere, He will back us up. God is good and faithful, but His manifestation comes supernaturally to those who follow and wait on the Lord.

Obedience is often not pleasing to our flesh and mind, but in the end, it bears the fruit of peace that glorifies the Lord. It says of Jesus in the book of Hebrews that because of what He suffered, He learned to obey.

"And though he was a son, yet by what he suffered he learned obedience." (Hebrews 5:8)

This flesh does not want to obey, but when we draw near to God and yield to Him, even though our flesh trembles, the grace of the Father sustains us, and His love strengthens us. There is nothing better than feeling sustained by the Father's grace, knowing that we are not alone, that He is with us. Despite all our circumstances, we are supported and victorious. Glory to God! It is something that must be lived and cannot even be explained sometimes. That is why many people do not understand when they see a child of God with many challenges, and still that person can smile, with joy in their heart, hopeful and at peace, even though outwardly they are falling apart. It is the power of the Lord. He truly strengthens us if we take refuge in Him wholeheartedly. That little voice, quiet and delicate, never abandoned me. During the trials, if we do not faint and continue to believe and surrender, God will be with us and give us victory.

It is very important to remember this: *Jesus Christ already paid for you and me on the Cross, but we need to believe, receive, surrender, and walk in Him.*

My husband and I got through all the waiting and anxiety, above all the uncertainties and challenges, because the Lord was with us and we trusted and remained in Him. Whoever makes a request to immigration from any country is not sure of how long the process might take, because it depends on the authorities and what they consider.

Much less in my case, for obvious reasons that you already know. Dear reader, by faith, we were in the winning team with Jesus. We trust Him, despite all our weaknesses and challenges. There will be times of difficulty, even of doubt, of discouragement; but the Lord lifts us up, speaks to us, gives us His promises, teaches us, instructs us, corrects us. It's wonderful! His promises are for each of us, my dear reader.

God's Justice

After having submitted everything to demonstrate my rehabilitation, we only had to wait and maintain our confidence. We had done everything we could. But we continued to pray and agree with each other and people of faith, praying and fighting for our promises. This was such a difficult time; everything inside us wanted to lower our arms, but the Lord was, and still is, our strength.

The LORD is my light and my salvation; whom shall I fear? The LORD is the strength of my life; of whom shall I be afraid? (Psalm 27:1-2)

The devil's tantrum

After several long months of waiting, I received a phone call. I was preparing to go on a Christian campaign with a well-known African prophet and preacher who was visiting my country. During that activity, I worked as an English/Spanish interpreter at no cost. I did it willingly for the Lord and anyone in need. That morning, the phone rang. I answered and heard a furious voice on the other end. I noticed others were nearby as well. The man said to me in a harsh, sarcastic, and demeaning tone—his voice filled with anger—"Look, you who say you are saved and now try to justify yourself by saying that you are a Christian. I'm not a Christian; I'm a hard worker, and my family has never had to deceive anyone. I'm more Christian than you are." He shouted many other things in a burst of anger. He called me a criminal, told me, "All those who have been in prison hide behind Christianity," and used many more degrading words, appearing very enraged. I never knew who he was or why he called me, but I imagine he was someone involved in my case as an investigator, or just another schemer, or someone who hates me intensely. When he let me speak, I said, "Yes, I may have been all you're saying, but I repented from the heart and turned my life around. Thanks to God, He gave me a new life and forgave me. Jesus has changed my life, and now I am no longer the person you are talking about; I have a new life because of His mercy." That man continued to say all the hurtful words he could, treating me as a criminal or a person who is good for nothing. Humbly, I said to him, "I pray that you and your family, if you have a mother, sister, wife, or daughters, never have to go through all the things I've gone through in my life." I continued, "I don't hide from what I was, but I also don't hide from what I am now, a new woman by the grace of God. My past does not define my future." I went on to tell him, "I'm glad your family is decent, hardworking, and good, but I'm going to remind you of what Jesus said *to the woman caught in adultery:*

"Let him who is without sins cast the first stone."

So, if you're free of sins, keep throwing stones at me." I had an emotional lump in my throat when I said it, and I wanted to cry so badly. But I refrained from doing so. I had finished speaking when that man hung up the phone harshly, which rang like an electric shock in my eardrum. I recovered and continued to prepare for my service to the Lord in the campaign. I left the house and participated in the campaign, empowered by the Holy Spirit and motivated by the love of God to serve with all my strength and love. Only the Holy Spirit can do that within us.

About a week later, I received the good news that I had been approved and welcomed into the nation of Canada. Glory to my Father! They sent me permission to enter and get my residency. Praise God, hallelujah! My Father is good and faithful! Thank you, Jesus! Glory to God! During those days, I was very sure that everything would be alright.

We had already managed to overcome stage one, proving that our marriage was legal and genuine, and now the second case was also approved. Jesus was glorified because He knows me from the depths of my heart and was there through my trials. Glory to the Father for that assurance in my heart, and by His Holy Spirit. He gives us His strength and His faith to be able to believe and to see His manifestation. Hallelujah!

Amid all the enemy's tantrums and using that person to defame me, I realized that before you receive the manifestation of your blessing, Satan tries to tempt you to abandon the path of faith and become discouraged. He urges you to leave your position and focus, convincing you that you will not be able to achieve what the Lord has promised. He brings all kinds of accusations, discouragements, attempts to offend you, and more. The devil is a liar, the father of all lies. Even if everything seems dark and tells you that it can't be or that you won't get there, God has promised to guide you and take you there; He will fulfill it. He is faithful, and He will bring you to where He promises, in His time, and depending on your yielding, in whatever He has given you in His Word.

Devil, I've been redeemed!

The devil gets angry when he doesn't achieve his goal, but I have been redeemed. I forgive my enemies, as God has forgiven me, and I pray for them. God does not leave His true children in shame. He fights for us. I faced many disadvantages with the system, but my old legal case ended at the Cross, more than 35 years ago when I received Christ. I have also borne many consequences for my actions and decisions. But God was and is my defender. He's the only one who knows my heart and is the one fighting for me, hallelujah! He also fights for you and has your case and needs in His hands. Trust in Him, my dear reader.

“He does not deal with man forever, nor forever keep anger.” (Psalms 103:9)

Colossians 2:14-15

Having abolished the written record of ordinances that were against us, which stood contrary to us, he (Jesus) took it away and nailed it to the cross, 15 and having disarmed the powers and authorities, he made a public spectacle of them, triumphing over them in it.

He is not mad with us; he loves us, and he wants the best for us.

The answer finally came

At the end of 2017, the answer finally arrived. I received a letter that said, "Congratulations, your case has been accepted and proven to have been rehabilitated, and we welcome you to Canada." I burst into tears of joy, my heart full of gratitude to my God. I jumped for happiness. It was a dream come true. I told my husband, who also jumped with excitement and gratitude. That man was ready to get his wife from the Dominican Republic immediately! Me! He came to my country for only 3 days. I told my church leaders that I was leaving, and they prayed for me and sent me away with blessings. They held a small party with lots of blessings, gifts, and food, wishing Donald and me joy and peace and prophesying about our future.

These words came from someone I love in the Lord when I let him know I was leaving: "You will do well, my sister."

I remembered what the prophet Isaiah said in chapter 3:10: *"Tell the righteous that it will be well with him, that he/she will eat of the fruit of his works."*

Chapter 16
Finally entering Canada

My husband flew to the Dominican Republic on Valentine's Day 2018 to get his beloved, and three days later, we flew together to Canada. Our flight lasted around 10 hours, and I couldn't sleep on the plane. I was struggling with my thoughts and worrying about how the Customs officers would treat me. I needed to control my emotions and mostly prayed during the flight. What would I face upon entering this new country? When I first set foot in Canada, I prayed and recited the words of Isaiah 3:10: "Say to the righteous, it will be well with them, for they will enjoy the fruit of their deeds." I received that Scripture from God through a leader in my home country before I left my country. When I arrived in Canada, the first thing I did was to bless the land and its inhabitants. Finally, I went through the security doors, and they guided us to a separate room to review everything with me and handle all the paperwork. They asked a few questions, and praise be to my Father, everything went smoothly. I enter with blessings into my new country that had received me with a clean record, just as the Lord received me and gave me a clean record because of the blood of Jesus and his great love. I walked through that gate as a daughter of the King. My husband's daughter and her family were waiting for me. They brought signs to the airport: "Welcome Joselyn, we love you. Welcome to your new family." They got me a thick winter coat as it was a cold winter month. I was so joyful and thankful to the Lord, my husband and this country that gave me another chance in life. Canada is a big and beautiful country.

It is great to see our prayers answered! It seemed to me as if I were dreaming. My beloved husband was thrilled. For a few days, we lived with

Donald's daughter, Crystal and her husband, Leo. Then we moved into a rented condo. Don sold the previous house he owned, paid off some debt, and had $3,000 left after paying it all off. We agreed to sow those three thousand dollars to the Lord as a special offering for all His goodness to us. We wanted to buy our house, but we couldn't, so we decided to sow that seed for the Lord and His work. The Lord, in less than a year, provided for a down payment on our house. It was a new house, modern and cozy. He opened doors for us and supplied us with so many other things that, if I continue, I will have to write another book. Hallelujah!

I came to Canada also to serve the Lord

When some of my friends knew that I was leaving my home country, they advised me, "Joselyn, take a few months, maybe a sabbatical year, so that you can get to know the country and enjoy it, and you and your husband can be together."

Donald was already a member of a local church, and I had already been in touch with those pastors before I came. They were praying for us. I couldn't wait or take a sabbatical as my friends suggested. We went to worship and thanked the Lord just a few days after I came. Within a few weeks of being here, I started serving, giving by grace what I received by grace. In a short time, I was entrusted with the task of leading a prayer group in that church. The pastor's wife, my dear Katie, and I became very good friends. She is with the Lord now. I remember her with love. I was invited to give my testimony and did the best I could. It was the first time I had given my testimony in English. It was in Church in the Vine, in Edmonton. I was nervous and praying in the spirit. I knew that being nervous with poor English is not a good combination. Haha. But my love for Jesus and souls had given me the courage to bear witness to His love, and to provide, serve, make sacrifices, broken English and all. Glory to God! I have asked the Lord for boldness. After two months of being in

Canada, I began to visit the prisoners. I went to witness and pray with the prisoners or share with them.

The cold weather is no joke, and coming from a very hot and tropical climate, it was not easy for me to adapt. As I write this, I am in my seventh year of living in Canada. I have adapted somewhat to the cold. I went through many changes in my life because of the extremely cold weather, especially here in Alberta, where we live. I needed to work, but instead of working right away, I wanted to explore Canada, meet its people, and learn about its culture. I also needed a job that felt meaningful to me. I prayed and looked for a career focused on helping others, because that's what I love. I enrolled in college and decided to become a Community Support Worker, which involves social work across different areas, supporting and helping people, working with individuals, groups, seniors, youth, newcomers, families, assistance agencies, addictions, and more. I studied very hard because my English isn't perfect, and I had to read many books, do homework, handle materials, practise, and present in front of my classmates, all in English. I had to study each lesson several times to understand it and get good results. A few years ago, I attended college classes while I was incarcerated, but I didn't finish the Associate of Arts program because it was time for me to leave the facility. I needed to go.

I also finished the Bible Institute (Bible College) the same year I got married, in 2013, back home. It was a blessing for me to graduate of an Associate in Practical Ministry.

By the time I started school again in Canada, I was returning to pursue a regular career at age 55 and in English. And there I was, like a young girl, who went to school full-time all day. I was a wife, involved in my church, serving God, and with daily classes, homework, presentations, and weekly exams. It was a condensed and very intense program. In the end, my scores were mostly A's, and my final score for the program was 90%. I prayed like crazy for the Holy Spirit to help me with all those classes, exams, and presentations. Thank You Jesus!

I graduated from college

The day of my graduation arrived, my son Jesse came from the United States, and along with my husband and stepdaughter, I received my diploma. It was a blessed day that filled me with gratitude, because this was something I wanted to do. I could have continued with a higher university career. I would have achieved it if I focused on it, because when I dedicate myself to doing something with the help of Christ, I can achieve it. But instead, at this moment in my life, more than university studies, I feel a call from God to take care of the things of the Kingdom of God, which is what I enjoy the most.

I am a prophetic intercessor and prayer warrior, and there is a call to evangelism. There is a burning desire to preach Jesus, the Kingdom, God's love and power to people. I have witnessed how many have come to Christ, have been reconciled to Him, or are encouraged and edified to believe and receive from the Lord. I have seen the Lord's mercy and grace first in my own life, and by seeing many receive Christ, be healed, and set free by the Lord, using me in unusual ways, glory to His Name. All honour, glory, and praise to the Great and Mighty God of whom I serve. Within a few months of graduating, I found my first job. I was employed in a company where I worked with people with disabilities and mental health problems. I am still working for the same company to this day.

With boldness, I testify of Christ

I began to preach in Canada, with great courage, willing to give by grace what I have received by grace. I stand in pulpits and bring out what I have inside. When God's presence touches us while preaching, we become unstoppable, despite all our flaws and humanity. Thanks to the Holy Spirit.

To the Lord be all glory. At first, it wasn't easy for me to adapt to this new culture. Everything was new to me here.

Where I live, there are not many people from my culture. But my love for God and His people has always driven me to meet people and has given me His grace to love and connect with people easily, regardless of race, colour, or nation. Human beings are God's creation, and the kingdom consists simply in loving God and loving people. I have many people around me who have blessed my life; some for a time or a season, and others who will be forever. There are so many precious people for whom I am grateful to the Lord. God has given me the gift of helping, and I am passionate about serving. I love to help others that God sends across my path, especially the neediest, who have no way to return a favour. The dedication and willingness to serve have allowed me to meet people from different nations, customs, languages and races, in many cases very different from me culturally; that is the Kingdom, we are all different but united by a great Lord. With God's love, I have been able to get along with them, and I have had the opportunity to show the Lord's love and sow seeds of faith in their lives, pray for them, or testify about the Lord's goodness and mercy. Many have come to know Jesus. Others have been edified, healed, delivered, or encouraged by the power of God. To Him be all glory, honour and grace, because we are His instruments.

I still receive reports from people who were imprisoned with me, and who are now free and born-again, praising Jesus for what He has done in their lives. The Lord used us to bring others to Him or to encourage them to persevere in Him. They are testimonies of His mercy throughout their lives. I have shared Jesus with many people from different countries and backgrounds—people from the Dominican Republic, Colombia, El Salvador, Puerto Rico, Mexico, Honduras, Haiti, Guatemala, Venezuela, the United States, the Philippines, and various parts of Africa. Jesus loves people; the Kingdom of God is about souls, so I also love souls. No matter our colour, language, culture, customs, or if they are different from me in the way they live or worship. I pray and trust the Lord for a harvest in the end times, and I will continue to preach and witness here in Canada and wherever He sends me. I will always be a witness for Jesus Christ. I am grateful for His love, mercy, grace, and power in my life, and for those He places around me. I owe everything to the Lord.

I identify myself with the woman at the well in John chapter 4.

Jesus came for the little ones, for the sick, not for the healthy (spiritually speaking), but for sinners, not for those who think they are righteous and healed.

The Samaritan woman was considered inferior because of her sex. She had a history of sexual relations with several men, but none of that mattered to Jesus because He saw her need for salvation and deliverance. After meeting Jesus, she ran to tell the people of her village about Jesus. They received her testimony and respected her, and they went with her to learn more about the Master. She became an evangelist.

I also identify with the woman who washed and anointed Jesus' feet during a banquet at the home of a Pharisee named Simon, in Luke 7:47-49. Jesus said to Simon after he questioned Jesus in his thoughts, saying, "*If Jesus were God, he would indeed know who he is dealing with" (paraphrased).*

Jesus turned to him and said, "I tell you, your many sins have been forgiven, so she has shown me much love. But a person who is forgiven little shows little love." Then, he said to the woman, "Your sins have been forgiven." In verse 50, Jesus said to the woman: "Your faith has saved you, go in peace."

Glory to God! What a precious gift it is to be forgiven and to have a new life through Jesus and in Him! My friends, truly, He is worthy of all our praise. I have heard the saying, "If you do not know my history, you will not understand my praise." That rings very true in my life. In the end, everything worked out for the best. The Lord has healed me, set me free, and given me a new identity as I build my character in Him. The Holy Spirit guides and affirms my life. Every day, I keep my heart and eyes fixed on Him, no matter what. He is faithful and cares for His children. He provided everything we need on the Cross, but we must collaborate, take up our cross, follow Him, and deny ourselves.

To serve is a privilege

I am so thankful to the Lord for the opportunity to start over in Canada. It's hard to start over, especially in a different nation and culture, but the Holy Spirit helps us, guides us, and supplies us. I thank the Lord for the restoration and restitution in my new nation. I have had the privilege of serving and volunteering in different ministries since I arrived six years ago. I have served by visiting the prisoners, leading a prayer group, and ministering in a drug rehabilitation program for about two years, where I learned even more about the damage and destruction caused by addictions and the world of drugs. God's power has also been manifested in ministering His love and mercy to the many women whom we have encountered. I have the privilege to serve in the children's ministry in my local churches, Champion City Church and I enjoyed it very much. I learn a lot from children, and I also receive their love. Children are great teachers. Currently, my husband and I are serving in our local church, and I also serve as a prayer warrior at the altar. I am a preacher as well, and I will continue to preach Jesus wherever I go or wherever He sends me. One of my strongest passions is prayer. I have the gift of edification and encouragement, and I love to inspire people to believe, rise, grow, be blessed, and glorify Jesus in their lives. I am willing to go where the Lord sends me and to be a witness for Him.

My husband Don and I have been married for 12 years. As I now translate and adapt the English version of my book (the original is in Spanish), we continue to depend on Jesus Christ. We love each other and, above all, respect one another. He recognizes God's call on my life and supports me because he is also part of God's plan. I thank God for him and our families. We keep believing the Lord for our children, grandchildren and families, and the purpose of God for our lives. We trust that God will fulfill His purpose in our children. We thank the Lord for them and believe that He will carry out His good plan for them and their descendants, In Jesus' name, we believe what the Word of the Lord says: *"Your children are a heritage of the LORD; and the fruit of the womb is his reward." (Psalm 127:3)*

We have five children altogether, three from him and two from me and eight grandchildren. We live by faith and not by sight. For both of us, our past doesn't define us. To the Lord, our sins and our past are forgiven and forgotten. We need to believe and yield. The Holy Spirit guides us every day in our marriage, and when we need alignment and help, every couple needs the intervention of the Lord. We all face challenges, and we all need help at one time or another, but now we are doing it with Jesus, and depending on Him, and not in ourselves. My past is no longer painful or shameful. I don't live a double-minded life, and I don't have a desire to do anything consciously that is outside of God's will.

Neither my husband nor I are yet perfect; none of us is, but the perfect one is in our midst as a Mighty Warrior. His name is Jesus Christ, our Saviour and Lord, the One who has never left us nor forsaken us and will continue to guide us, help us, and lift us.

My heart is healthy and sensitive to the Kingdom of God and His righteousness. I long more for Him and Him alone. I give all the glory and honour to Him. Jesus Christ is Lord and King; His Name is above all other names.

A call for you, my reader

Like many today, you might be reading this book and wanting to learn more about Jesus. Perhaps you need Him in your heart today. Maybe you need to return to Him, or you desire more of Him; you need to surrender all to Him. I want to remind you that He loves you and cares about you. He is the One who has given purpose to my life and has granted me a new life. He is the One who has restored me. He will be there for you if you surrender and give your life to Him. If you need to come to Him today, or if you have known Him before but are now far from Him, it is a new day for you. Reach out to Him. Pray this prayer with all your heart if you need to receive Him.

*"**God, I know I'm a sinner, and I need You to forgive me. Please forgive me. I accept Jesus Christ as my Lord and Saviour today. Jesus, enter my heart, cleanse me with your blood shed on Calvary, teach me and guide me. Today, I believe and declare that you are the Lord of my life. My life from today on is yours. Thank you for dying for me, for forgiving me, accepting me, and loving me. Amen.**"*

Or if you need to reconcile or yield, pray the following:

Say with all your heart, "*Lord, here I am. Forgive me for all my transgressions and sins. I yield to you, help me to do Your will, and lead me in the paths of righteousness. I detach myself from all rebellion, iniquities, pride and darkness. I break all relationships with the enemy, and I return to you. Holy Spirit, come and fill me.* *Amen.*"

Don't stop gathering, attend a sound doctrine, church, or community to fellowship. Read His Holy Word and talk to God. Seek His Kingdom. May His healing, love, fresh anointing, and strength touch you, heal you, free you, and encourage you today, beloved reader. May the Lord meet you at the point of your needs and reveal Himself to you.

I bless you. Amen.

Praise for God's Blessings

Psalm of David 103

Bless the Lord, oh my soul, and bless my whole being his holy name. Bless the Lord, O my soul,

And don't forget any of its benefits.

He is the one who forgives all your iniquities, the one who heals all your infirmities.

He who rescues your life from the pit,

The one who crowns you with favours and mercies; the one who satisfies your mouth well, so that you may be rejuvenated like the eagle."

"Therefore, if anyone is in Christ, he is a new creation; old things have passed away; behold, all are made new." (2 Corinthians 5:15)

Dear reader, it's never too late.

You're never too far away to get up, come to the Father, and start fresh. It's never too late to hold God's hand and try once more time in what you feel isn't working or seems impossible. Come on, rise and shine!

"For God, there is nothing impossible." (Luke 1:37)

Thank You, My Lord Jesus Christ. I owe everything to You. I worship You and bow down before You. I love You, Lord. Here I am, Father.

For prayer or contact

Joselyn Joaquin Jenkins

Facebook: @joselynjoaquin

Instangram: @joselynjenkins Youtube: @joselynjoaquin

Website:https://www.joselynjenkin.com/

Escribenos a: contact@joselynjenkins.com

My dear reader, next, I am sharing some pictures of my life's journey with you; they are not the best pictures that I have taken, but they are meaningful to me.

Thank you for reading my history. God bless you.

MY mother and father

I was a year here

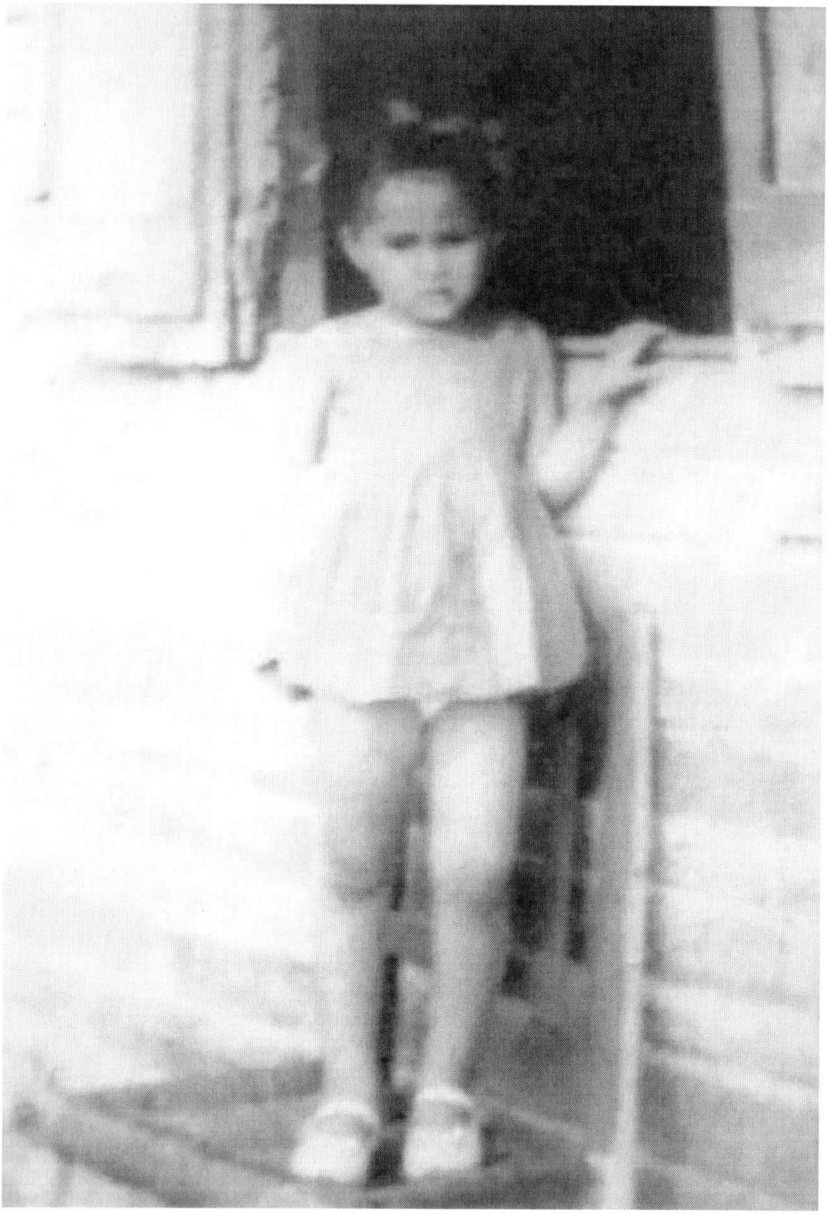

In my grandmother's house

Me 4 years. My sister Lourdes 2

What I love to do, Reading. 13 years old

My teens years

My father.

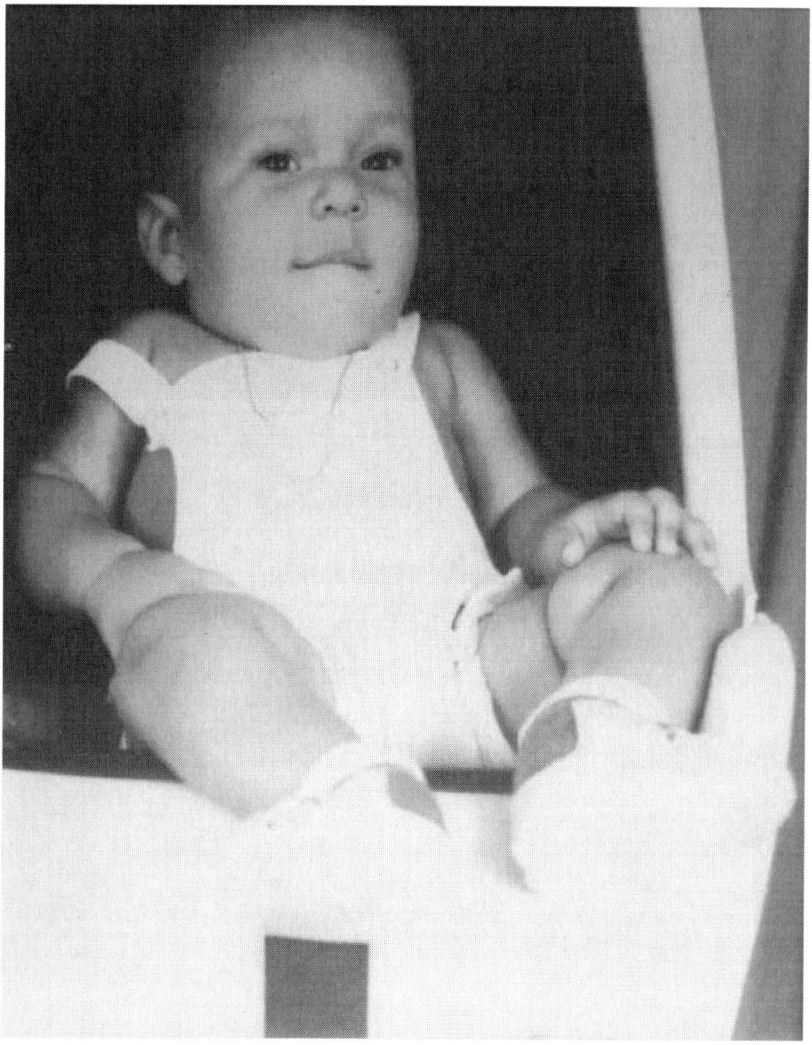

My son Aneurys, first year

When I used to visit my mother,

In the choir, Florida State Institution, 1991

Jesse is visiting me in/Federal prison.

My sister and Jesse, visiting -Federal Institution

My GED graduation in prison

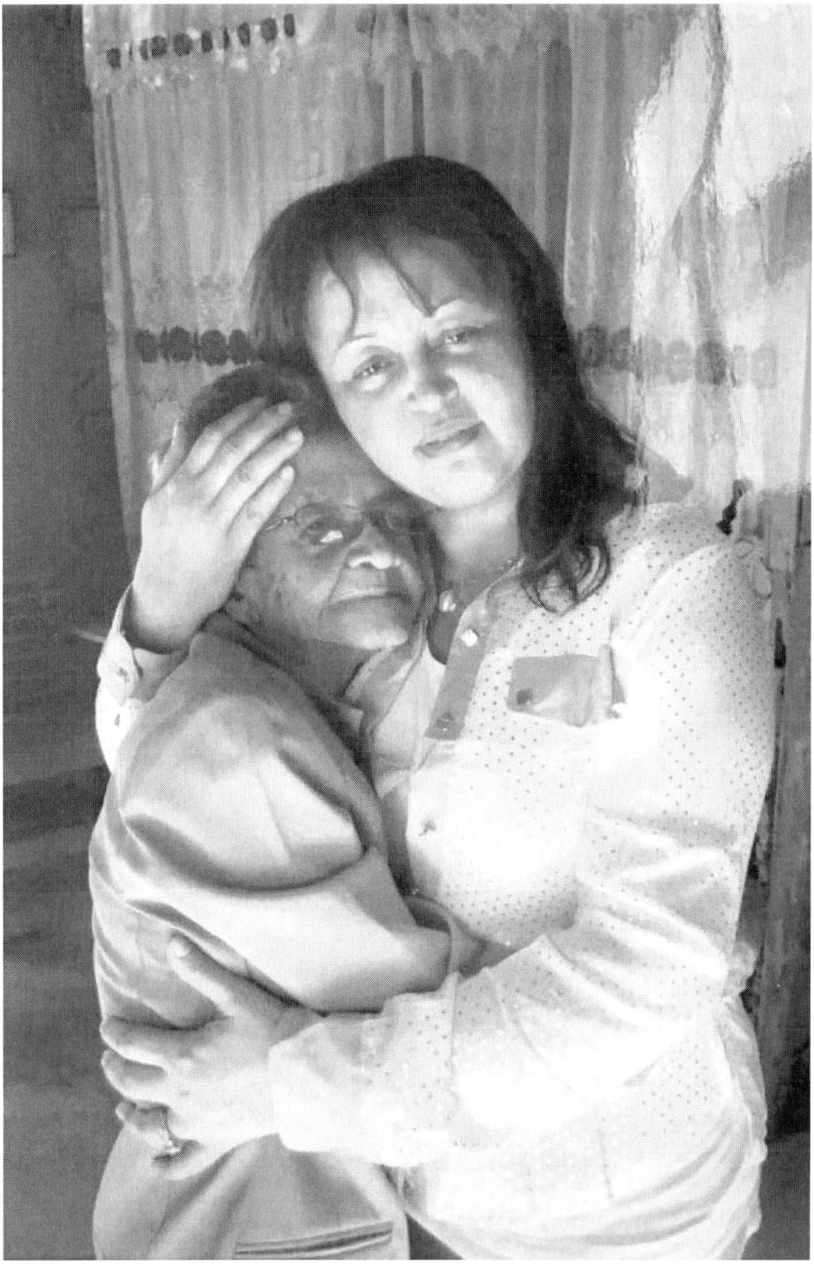

My grandmother Flora in her last days

My grandfather Cristino and my grandmother Flora

Grandmother and my mother

My mother and most of my brothers and sisters

Brother and sisters from my mother

Celebrating Mother's Day. My son Aneurys, first grandson Gabriel and my daughter-in-law Inmaculada.

Don and I dating

My beautiful Lady and I

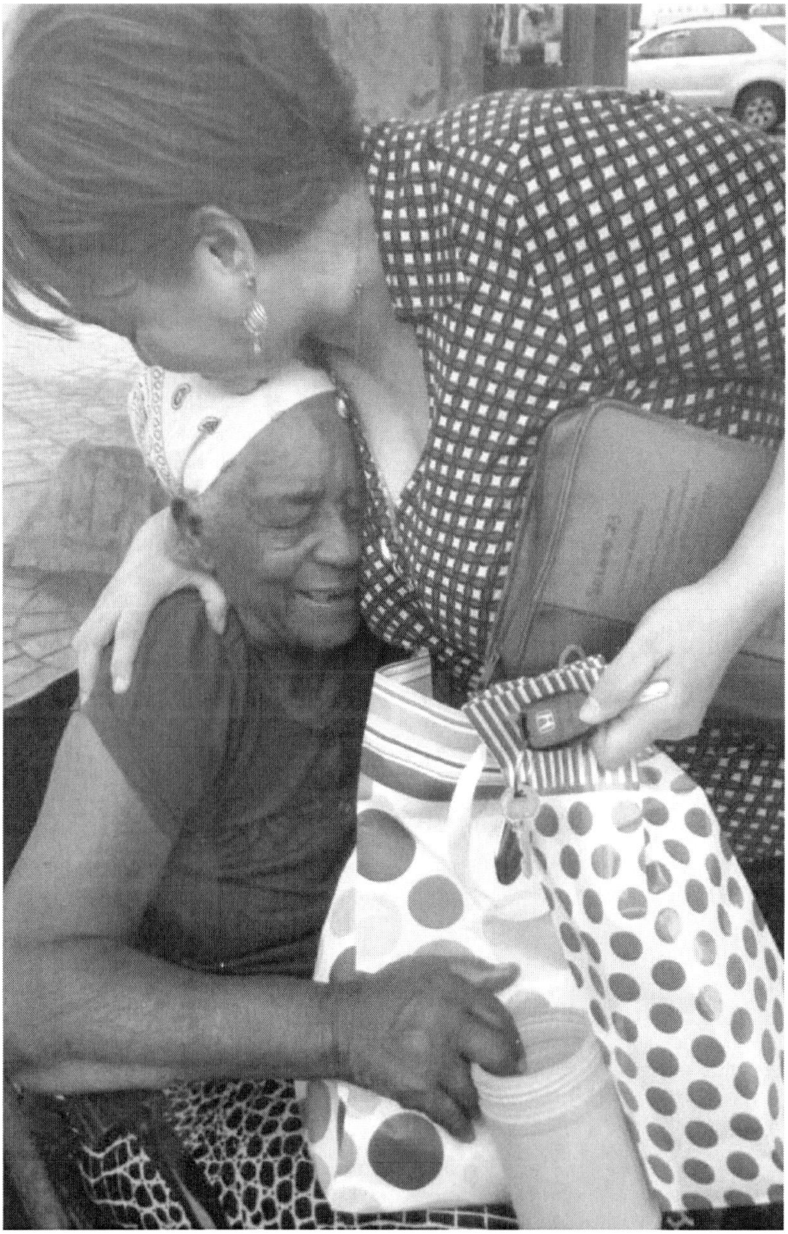

Serving the Lord on the streets. A beautiful soul
to remember and a reminder for me.

Hereafter, I graduated from Radio Broadcasting-transmitting.

My graduation- As a Broadcaster 2016

My marriage in church, Dec 2013, with my pastors
Apostle Miguel Bogaert and Prophet Montserrat Bogaert

Wedding: My nephew Ronald, Niece Kiara, and
Grandson Gabriel as my pages

My mother supper happy

He and I and my snow-white dress lol

Civil ceremony 2013

My Best man-my son Aneurys, here with my nice, grandson and nephew

Graduation from Bible Institute 2013

Entering Canada for the first time.

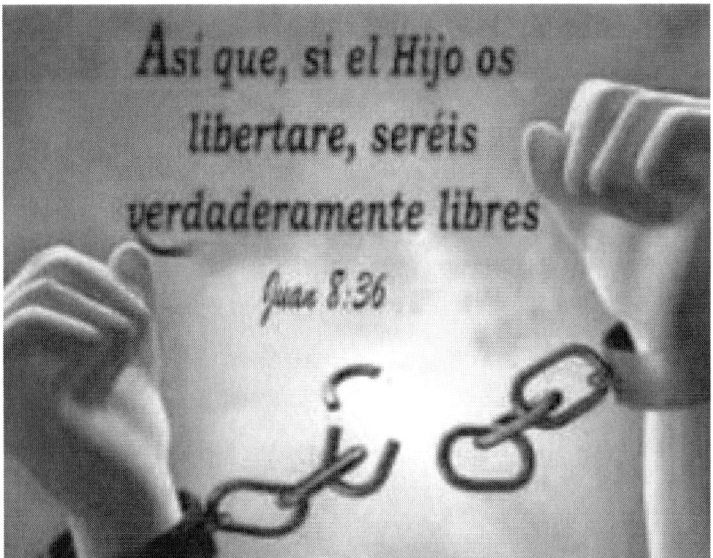

If the Son of man set you free, you are free indeed. John 8:36

Final day in College, Community Support Worker graduation in Canada

Graduation

Preaching to Women in Canada Church in the Vine

My Lord deserves all praise.

First visit to Canada of my son Jesse

Giving by grace

First time giving my testimony in English, Church in the Vine, Edmonton- Canada

Volunteer appreciation. A hug that means a great deal to me.

My pastors, Dean and Laura Forster-Champion City Church

One of our granddaughters Celine.

Canada family

Family in Canada

The day that I became a Canadian-gloria a Dios.

Celine and I

Lake Louise, Canadá.

Went back to visit Dominican Republic in 2022. My 2 children and us.

My children and 2 grandchildren, Gabriel and Gael, in Dom. Rep.

Preaching - Canadá.

We are and will be grateful to the Lord Jesus Christ forever

7

Manufactured by Amazon.ca
Acheson, AB

30367901R00136